THE SEXUAL INTEGRITY WORKBOOK

SOLUTION-FOCUSED TOOLS FOR LASTING FREEDOM FROM PROBLEMATIC SEXUAL BEHAVIOR

BLAIR P. BISHER

Copyright © 2026 by Blair P. Bisher

All rights reserved.

No part of this book may be reproduced in any form or by any electronic or mechanical means, including information storage and retrieval systems, without written permission from the author, except for the use of brief quotations in a book review.

If you always do what you've always done you'll always get what you've always got.

HENRY FORD

It's only after we've lost everything that we're free to do anything.

CHUCK PALAHNIUK

They can because they think they can.

VIRGIL

The best time to plant a tree is 20 years ago, the second best time is now.

CHINESE PROVERB

If the rule you followed brought you to this, of what use was the rule?

ANTON CHIGURH, NO COUNTRY FOR OLD MEN

I'm not who I want to be, but I'm not who I used to be.

JOHN NEWTON

CONTENTS

Preface	vii
1. The Sustainability Formula	1
Motivation + Value = Sustainability	
2. Do I Have a Problem?	3
Problematic Sexual Behavior	7
Problematic Porn Consumption Scale	10
Goal Setting	12
Primary Presenting "Problem"	16
Your behavior makes sense... or else you're nonsensical.	
3. Becoming a Self-Expert	18
Sobriety is cheap. Sustainability is everything.	
Daily Check-in	20
Relapse Prevention Plan	23
It is impossible to hate yourself into healthy	
4. Your Relapse Prevention Plan	25
The Three Circles Exercise	40
Inner, Middle & Outer Circles	
5. Feelings, Consequences, History & Pathology	43
Recovery Timeline	52
6. Process	55
The Biggest Little Word in Behavior Change	
7. The Addiction Cycle	66
Answering the 'Why'	
Self-Application: Addiction Cycle	74
Defense Mechanisms	80
Answering "How could you do that?!"	
Intrinsic Motivation	86
8. Are You in Control?	88
Who gets to dictate terms - you or your emotions?	
9. Shame & Internalization	92
10. Safe Vulnerability	99
"Is it Safe to be Me?"	
11. The Role of Intimacy	104
12. Beware Recovery Fatigue	112
The Law of Diminishing Returns	
Final Thoughts	113
Your Notes	115
Feel Free to take as many notes as you'd like in this section	

Daily Check-In Template	127
About the Author	129
References	131

PREFACE

Observation Before Operation.

∼

In case you missed it...
　　OBSERVATION BEFORE OPERATION.

∼

I've had a wild career. In one role I worked the night shift in an Emergency Room at a level 1 Trauma center where my tiny one-chair office overlooked the ER waiting room. One notable observation I made during that time was that people overwhelmingly rush into the ER having already diagnosed their 'primary presenting problem' and are eager to present the 'solution' as well. To be fair, many understandably are subject matter experts on themselves and are desperately trying to relive physical pain. However, to provide the greatest likelihood for a positive outcome, despite what the patient's lived experience has been, the best clinical path forward was to begin the enormous lift that is the triage, intake and observation process.

　　While the patient was strongly advocating for immediate surgery, the treatment team first had to obtain an incredible amount of data - name, age, date of birth, medical history, family history, allergies, etc. connected to this presenting discomfort, oxygen levels, A1C for the diabetics, full blood draw for labs, heart rhythm, blood pressure, weight, current medication regimen, possible imaging studies (X-Ray, Ultrasound, MRI or CT scan), talk to family members or healthcare power of attorney to understand the patient's wishes pertaining to DNR/DNI (do not resuscitate/do not intubate) and more.

99.9% of the time that patient was not rushed to the OR, but rather the patient was OBSERVED. Their results were monitored, further assessed, possible new tests ordered or questions asked. A warm blanket and a ginger ale were offered - likely running fluids for general hydration. In the overwhelming majority of cases this observation period determined that extreme measures (eg. surgery) were not necessary - sometimes it was - but most often not. This successful 'observation, not operation' treatment pathway was so common that a phrase arose:

ME: "DR. JONES, WHAT'S THE PLAN WITH MR. SMITH IN ROOM 4?"
MD: "METABOLIZE TO FREEDOM."

What this meant was that the patient needed to let the body do its thing whether it be to process newly onboarded medications, let the cold compress, IV, oxygen, sleep do its thing, and then they'd be on their way. This treatment pathway was greatly preferred as unnecessarily operating on the patient could cause considerably more pain/discomfort/destruction to them, even more than the presenting pain they were experiencing at admission.

Why do I share this story in particular?

If you are reading this book, I am to assume that you are presenting with mild to extreme emotional pain. Understandably, when we are in extreme discomfort or pain we all want relief as fast and effectively as possible in both medical/surgical environments as well as mental and behavioral health too. However, I would encourage you as you begin this workbook, DO NOT run to fix it mode, do not run to the operating room. First, we must OBSERVE. We must look, assess, test, poke, prod, ask a million questions, we desperately need to UNDERSTAND what it is that we're working with.

What this looks like in seeking sustainable sexual integrity, you're very likely trying to undo damage, hurt, pain that you and others you care very much about are experiencing. There is a burning house and you're racing for the fire hose - which is a sensible response. However, I'm proposing that rushing too quick to find a solution, to figure it out, to answer all of your partner's questions (many times on repeat) can be rushing to the OR with incomplete information. Operating with incomplete info leads to further complications we'd rather avoid and which will only set us further back.

Let us work together in this workbook to get to a level of self-expertise. It is in the increased and comprehensive understanding of pathological, destructive thought and behavior patterns that you can determine the correct treatment path. Slow down. Take a breath. We're going to be here for a minute. I can imagine that you, and possibly those you love, are very likely in many levels of pain currently - we're going to lean into it, we're not running from it because we're safe here. It's spicy, everything may be screaming for relief, and I will still propose that we are safe here. There is no better place to be than right here, showing up for yourself and your loved ones, showing up for your future self - there is no healthier place than where you are right at this very minute. Take a huge inhale in then breathe out (I'll wait). Actually, that was nice, take 2 more huge breaths in and then out...

You've got this. The human brain is amazing at acclimating to painful scenarios and it has already begun doing so for you in this time. And remember...
You are not alone. Your story is unique, but I promise you are not alone.

Levels of Care

The last thing I want to mention is this concept of 'levels of care.'
Sticking with the ER analogy, the Emergency Room is a specific level of care, meaning that we are starting at the most extreme treatment level needed at the moment. Immediately, though, the planning has already begun to move the patient out to a lower level of care that is more clinically appropriate. That may be to discharge home, maybe even the ER isn't enough and the patient needs to move quickly over to the ICU or possibly somewhere in-between the two, moved up to a general medical-surgical floor for further observation.

I would strongly recommend that you begin considering your recovery journey on this continuum of levels of care. Possibly today you're reading this from what feels like the ER. If you continue to engage and show up for yourself you will gradually move in the direction of discharge home.

This is incredibly important also when you (and possibly your partner) consider your 'process' which we discuss in detail in chapter 2. Process being the collection of things you do to move in a healthier direction. What your process looks like in the 'ER' compared to a lower level of care will be very different - and appropriately so. Lower acuity means less intervention, less hands-on needed. This progression via improvement over time can terrify you and your partner as it seems you're 'losing interest' in recovery work, however, I would propose that is not the case at all. That if you continue to show up for yourself your plan will adapt to your appropriate level of care, or clinical need, at that time.

The things you may be doing every single day now, you should not be doing every single day one year from now. As your level of acuity decreases, your awareness and healing progresses, the need for your brain and body will also change and this progression is to be celebrated not harangued over. It's success, not concern. Consider adding this question into your regular check-in: 'what level of care am I currently?'

1

THE SUSTAINABILITY FORMULA
MOTIVATION + VALUE = SUSTAINABILITY

While self-expertise offers the greatest opportunity for sustainable sexual integrity, it is also a long road with no clear endpoint.

To help jumpstart your recovery journey, I offer a quick-acting simplified formula distilled over time reflecting on the inverse of sustainability - or anti-sustainability (or frequent relapse) - and what drives it. I would propose that relapse occurs when one of two things is lost:

1. Motivation (your 'why')
2. Value - you stop finding value in previously helpful recovery activities

Motivation

If your motivation for getting this book is to restore your marriage, this is your clear 'why.' Why set aside time every day to consider, process, be intentional, confront your belief structure, work to identify your emotions, practice journaling, write gratitude lists, etc? Why do all that? Well, something like keeping your family together is a great motivator for many, understandably.

So, what happens when you're successful? All good things, right?? You are able to demonstrate growth, transparency, self-awareness, empathy, vulnerability and so both you and your partner move forward with your relationship - this is wonderful! However, I'd propose it also carries a degree of risk as you have now lost your primary motivator of restoring your marriage appears satisfied, so for great reason your motivation has been lost. What will motivate you know that your primary motivator has been achieved?

Often times, relapse occurs once incredible achievements have occurred as motivation has been satiated and not supplanted intentionally with another.

As you begin to develop your unique check-in regimen with yourself, consider adding this motivation consideration as a part of it.

Value

What are the activities you're engaging in where you find value being added to your life? You wake up excited to participate in them. It could be journaling, taking a walk, your morning hot shower or hot cup of coffee, checking in with your partner, pastor, sponsor, friend, playing with your dog or feeding your turtle. It can also be specifically tied to your sobriety process, gratitude lists, attending therapy/meeting/group, setting an intention for the day, tracking disruptive thoughts or core beliefs.

Either way, as you engage in your journey, it is incredibly important to discover activities in which you genuinely find they are adding value to your life and/or process.

Now, having discovered such wonderful value-added work/moments in your life, fully anticipate that the very things you find incredibly helpful today will not feel as beneficial in 90 days' time. In twelve months time you may find that literally everything you started out doing at the beginning feels like a chore. There's nothing wrong with you, you've not 'lost interest' per se, but rather as with most things in life our brain and body will acclimate - thankfully.

This is also referred to as 'Recovery Fatigue' which we'll discuss further in chapter 10.

FOOD FOR THOUGHT

- What is your motivation currently? Has it changed over time?
- What would likely cause you to lose your current motivation?
- Where are you finding incredible value in your routines? What could likely decrease that value over the next 6 months?
- Consider these factors in your efforts and you may quite well defend against unnecessary relapse.

2

DO I HAVE A PROBLEM?

IF YOU'RE ASKING 'DO I HAVE A PROBLEM?' THE ANSWER IS 'YES.'

The reason being is that you have now moved out of 'pre-contemplation' and into 'contemplation.' A moment ago, you were not even considering the possibility of a problem of any sort, thus the very shift in thinking to 'Do I have a problem?' is a shift into contemplation as we understand the transtheoretical model of behavior change (Raihan & Cogburn, 2023).

Recovery from addiction starts with a recognition and acknowledgment of the addiction itself. Because of the social stigma surrounding both sex and porn addiction, it's often difficult to recognize when one reaches the level of problematic sexual behavior. Compulsive or "problematic" sexual behavior is generally defined as repeated sexual behavior that hinders daily functioning or emotional well-being. Many with compulsive or problematic sexual behavior patterns feel incapable of "stopping" their actions, despite harmful effects on their quality of life and/or relationships.

Sex addiction, pornography addiction, repeated infidelity and compulsive masturbation are all examples of problematic sexual behavior. Each involves a personal tension with recurrent sexually-motivated thoughts, impulses, and actions. Often, this behavior is perpetuated as an attempt to self-regulate (or self-medicate) difficult emotions. Self-regulation by way of acting out is where one engages with the problematic behavior as a tool to relieve (numb, avoid, escape) difficult, or unwanted, emotions. This is not just an escapism from reality, but much more severe as this is an attempted escape from yourself. This pattern is reinforced and thus embedded over time as the 'problem' becomes 'the solution' to the brain by way of the 'relief reward.'

> "Neuroscience research has revealed that addiction is a chronic (...) disease of the brain triggered by repeated exposure (...) in those who are vulnerable because of genetics and developmental or adverse social exposures. As a result, the reward circuit's capacity to respond to reward and motivate actions that are not drug related is decreased, the sensitivity of the emotional circuits to stress is enhanced, and the capacity to self-regulate is impaired. The result is compulsive ... seeking and ... taking despite severe harms and an inability to control the strong urges to consume, even when there is a strong desire to quit." (Volkow et al., 2019)

Breaking free from this reward pattern can be difficult, but it is entirely possible.

To simplify things a bit, consider four things:

1. Mood Regulation — Engaging in an activity with the intent to "feel better" is a natural instinct. It can be a wonderful thing: a hot shower, cold drink in the summer, hugging a loved one, taking a nap, a great workout. These are all examples of healthy mood regulation. However, some attempts to regulate your mood can be unhealthy and detrimental. Needing a drink to relax, using porn to "escape" for a bit, masturbating for stress relief. Are you engaging in problematic behaviors expressly to improve your mood?

2. Negative Consequences — Doing something to regulate your mood that does not result in negative consequences is, by definition, not problematic. Taking a hot bath at the end of a long day is not problematic, as you are unlikely to receive negative consequences by doing so. However, if you take so many hot baths that your water bill becomes unaffordable, your attempt at mood regulation has resulted in negative consequences. Have you experienced negative consequences as a result of your preferred mood-regulating behaviors?

3. Unmanageability — When an attempt at mood regulation results in negative consequences, the logical action is to set boundaries to avoid repetition. For the bath, your boundary might be, "I am only going to take four baths a week, so as not to generate an obscenely high electric/water bill." Then, if you find yourself taking two baths a day, unable to keep your self-established boundary and are subsequently unable to pay your bills, the behavior has become problematic and the spiral of dysfunction begins. Has your pattern ever become unmanageable by way of violating your self-established boundaries?

4. Transparency - Possibly the most important of the four - Do you hide your behavior, cover your tracks, have a public/private persona split, or maybe there's no obvious attempt to hide but simply a desire to not have others become aware? This lack of transparency is often enough to supercede the previous items mentioned and indicate a problematic pattern. Have you hidden your problematic patterns for any reason?

Here, you'll complete the Bisher Addiction Brief Survey (BABS), a tool to help you evaluate and acknowledge your problem. This test has been designed for simplicity and clarity in identifying problematic behavior.

Bisher Addiction Brief Survey (BABS)

Mood Regulation
Do you engage in this behavior to feel better or less-worse?

Yes: ☐

No: ☐

Negative Consequences
Do you experience negative consequences as a result of this behavior?

Yes: ☐

No: ☐

Unmanageability
Are you unable to maintain the boundaries you set for yourself?

Yes: ☐

No: ☐

Lack of Transparency
Do you hide, cover-up, avoid detection relative to your patterns of behavior?

Yes: ☐

No: ☐

Yes to all four questions indicates severe problematic behavior, likely meeting the full criteria for addiction. **Yes** to 'lack of transparency' alone is also indicative.

Bisher Addiction Brief Survey (BABS)

"Do I have an addiction?"

'Yes' to all questions indicates problematic behavior. 'Yes' to only #4 may supercede all else.

01 Mood Regulation
You engage in the behavior to feel better or less worse.

02 Negative Consequences
You experience negative consequences as a result of the behavior.

03 Unmanageability
You set boundaries but cannot maintain them.

04 Transparency
You hide, cover up, deceive.

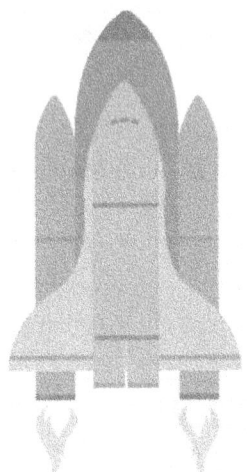

PROBLEMATIC SEXUAL BEHAVIOR

Various Types...

PORNOGRAPHY

One of the most prevalent struggles related to compulsive sexual behavior is an addiction to pornography. Porn addiction is considered a process addiction (Grant et al., 2010), often not formally recognized as a chemical addiction disorder, a growing number of people report symptoms and effects similar to those in other forms of chemical addiction. For reference, other forms of process addiction are work, shopping, etc. Some people can engage with pornography on a casual basis, avoiding the development of a dependency, while others find themselves suffering from compulsive and repetitive consumption, frequent cravings, and effects resembling withdrawal.

A primary defining element of porn addiction is a loss of control, or unmanageability. Someone in the midst of their addiction might continue their behavior despite wishing to stop, or experiencing negative effects caused by the addiction. An addiction to pornography does not indicate a lack of willpower or self-control. Rather, it indicates an underlying need thus driving a human struggle leading to a vicious cycle on inner-tension. The majority of people who self-report problematic porn usage feel distressed by their own behavior, many reporting previous attempts to "quit" with varying degrees of success.

Ultimately, porn addiction is characterized by consistent, compulsive consumption that persists despite negative consequences (harm inflicted upon one's own life, relationships, or mental well-being). The obsessive nature of addiction allows its effects to bleed into one's daily life. Somebody struggling with excessive porn usage may discover harm (destruction) caused to their marriage, career, and emotional state due to the pattern of behavior. This pain fosters an impulse to repeat the behavior rather than face the issue head-on (dysfunction). This pattern of destructive dysfunction will continue to play out until an intervening force is applied by self or others. We will talk more later about harm reduction as a method for sustainable sobriety (graphic below). Porn addiction, though commonly experienced but under-reported, is shrouded in stigma and lacking in open discussion (Grubbs et al., 2019). If you resonate with these characterizations, you may be "trapped" in the porn addiction cycle. The good news: nobody is ever trapped. You possess the strength and resilience to fully eliminate your addiction and grow into the life you want to be living. Before we can start to 'operate,' we must first observe and evaluate. The first step, of course, is to identify the problematic pattern itself.

The Problematic Pornography Consumption Scale (PPCS) is a tool used to evaluate a person's pornographic consumption and any potential detrimental effects. The elements in the scale measure how frequently pornography is consumed, how it affects a person's relationships and daily life, and how troubled they may feel as a result of their pornographic use. Numerous research studies have employed the PPCS to evaluate problematic pornography use and the potential harm it may cause to people.

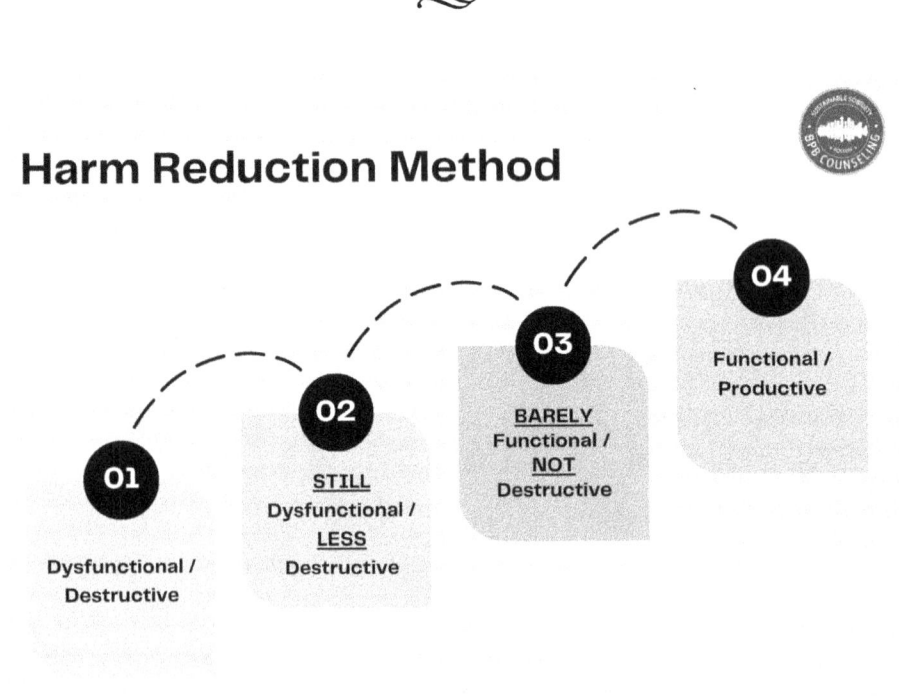

Other areas of of problematic sexual behavior that should be considered...

INFIDELITY

This typically presents as violation of a relationship contract. Whether it's emotional affairs, talking with strangers online, meeting in-person, varying degrees of sexual engagement - generally infidelity is determined as a violation of implicit or explicit relationship contract between parties. What those boundaries are, and how clear they are, varies by each relationship.

Simply put, what may be deemed infidelity in one relationship, such as scrolling social media 'thirst traps' may be perfectly fine in other relationships. Clearly defined boundaries are integral in helping to determine healthy paths forward and healing from betrayal.

TRANSACTIONAL INTIMACY

Pursuing intimacy in any arena that yields negative consequences and is being leveraged for the purposes of numbing, avoiding and escaping either chronic or acute stressors.

PORN-ADJACENT

Most often this looks like social media (SnapChat, Tik Tok, Instagram), reddit forum chat rooms, Facebook, taking pictures of others without their consent, etc. It is important to discuss these grey zones which will bring clarity.

ARTIFICIAL INTIMACY

AI companions has been skyrocketing in their popularity and adoption as well as Private Equity backing as a play to exploit the recent epidemic of societal isolation, loneliness and particularly male loneliness, all accelerating post-COVID lockdown.

The list of areas where sexual behavior can become problematic is virtually endless, which is why the Bisher Addiction Brief Survey was created in answering whether or not an obscure or outright pattern has become dysfunctional.

The Problematic Pornography Consumption Scale

The Problematic Pornography Consumption Scale (PPCS) is a tool used to evaluate a person's pornographic consumption and any potential detrimental effects. The elements in the scale measure how frequently pornography is consumed, how it affects a person's relationships and daily life, and how troubled they may feel as a result of their pornographic use. Numerous research studies have employed the PPCS to evaluate problematic pornography use and the potential harm it may cause to people (Beáta Bőthe et al., 2021).

Think back on the last six months and use the 7-point scale to indicate the extent to which each statement applies to you. There is no right or wrong answer.

∽

1. Never | 2. Rarely | 3. Occasionally | 4. Sometimes | 5. Often | 6. Very often | 7. All the time

Porn was an important part of my life.
1 ☐ ☐ ☐ ☐ ☐ ☐ 7

Porn caused problems in my sex life.
☐ ☐ ☐ ☐ ☐ ☐

I used porn to regulate my emotions.
☐ ☐ ☐ ☐ ☐ ☐

I had to watch more and more porn for the same satisfaction.
☐ ☐ ☐ ☐ ☐ ☐

I tried unsuccessfully to reduce my porn usage.
☐ ☐ ☐ ☐ ☐ ☐

I felt stressed when prevented from watching porn.
☐ ☐ ☐ ☐ ☐ ☐

I thought about how good it would be to watch porn.

PROBLEMATIC PORN CONSUMPTION SCALE

☐ ☐ ☐ ☐ ☐ ☐

Watching porn reduced my negative emotions.
☐ ☐ ☐ ☐ ☐ ☐

Watching porn prevented me from being my best self.
☐ ☐ ☐ ☐ ☐ ☐

I resisted watching porn before relapsing.
☐ ☐ ☐ ☐ ☐ ☐

I craved porn intensely when I didn't watch it for a while.
☐ ☐ ☐ ☐ ☐ ☐

I vowed to quit porn but only stopped for a short period of time.
☐ ☐ ☐ ☐ ☐ ☐

I became agitated when I was unable to watch porn.
☐ ☐ ☐ ☐ ☐ ☐

I consistently planned when to watch porn.
☐ ☐ ☐ ☐ ☐ ☐

I relieved tension by watching porn.
☐ ☐ ☐ ☐ ☐ ☐

I neglected other activities as a result of my porn usage.
☐ ☐ ☐ ☐ ☐ ☐

I gradually watched more "extreme" porn.
☐ ☐ ☐ ☐ ☐ ☐

For your total score, add up the numbers applied to each statement. A score of **76 or greater** suggests problematic pornography usage.

Total Score: _____

GOAL SETTING

GOAL SETTING

As you begin to structure your recovery plan, an easy way to get started is by setting your goals. Creating an outline of your aims allows you to envision your life post-recovery, providing a reminder of your "why" when things get tough. This outline also acts as a list of checkpoints to return to throughout your journey. Each personal goal you achieve will empower you to keep going. The goals you will be creating at the end of this chapter will be four things:

1. SMART
2. Long-term first
3. Clarified as Short-term
4. Positively framed

∼

LONG TERM

First by establishing where it is you would like to be in 3, 6, 12 and 36 months. Forget about HOW you do it, that's where the brain always gets held up, simply consider 'miracle state', what would you like it to look like regardless of the impossibility of conceiving it in today's setting. I can assure you that you will never get there - wherever it is you're going - if you cannot define the vision you're striving toward.

While you're 'miracle stating', do your best to not be encumbered with this idea of 'what you deserve.' Simply consider what it is that you would like to see in your life down the road.

A long-term goal should focus on **resolving** and **eliminating** the problem or **achieving** something. These goals represent the broader picture and your desired endgame. Ideally, as we'll look at next, your short-term goals will help determine our HOW, but long-term will more center on WHERE it is that we're trying to get.

You don't have to absolutely have a long-term goal, however, do the best you can otherwise this process will feel very much like a meandering in the wilderness for you and those who are hoping you find a healthier space for yourself.

SHORT TERM

Short-term goals should be targeted towards **reducing** and **relieving** the problem or simply **improving** or **increasing** a desired trait, routine etc. It's tempting to want to fix everything at once, but ultimately, it's more helpful to start out with realistic goals that lay a solid foundation for your recovery.

I'll just throw out my favorite short-term goal in here which is increased awareness. It's a short-term goal that almost no one ever selects, yet I believe it is one of the most fundamental, important and effective short-term goals. Again, that observation (understanding) before operation (fixing).

SMART

The most beneficial way to craft your goals is by remembering the components of a **SMART** goal.

SMART:
Specific
Measurable
Achievable
Relevant
Time-constrained

A SMART goal greatly increases your chance for success. These goals are much more realistic and attainable, increasing your ability to achieve them. Most failed goals are caused by setting an over-idealized goal, and while making progress, still walking away viewing themselves as a 'failure' thus driving the cycle of self-shame and acting counteractive to sustainable sobriety. A **SMART** goal paves the way for steady, realistic and sustainable growth.

It's worth noting that growth - unless you're Bernie Madoff - does not occur in a perfect linear fashion. There are going to be fits and starts, ups and downs, back and forth, growth and pain... many of these things happening at the same time. So, if we know that these things are a part of the growth and healing process then it is quite possible to reframe one's view of these bumps along the way as markers of progress. These 'wrinkles' are signs that you're engaging and attempting - which is always incredibly healthy, regardless of outcome on a certain and single point in time.

Lastly, if possible, remember to frame your goals positively - what is it that you WILL be doing. Often in recovery, goals begin negatively framed - what it is you DON'T want to be doing.

Bottom line, positively framed goals are statistically and significantly more likely to be achieved when compared to negatively framed goals (Tuk, 2024).

OUTLINE YOUR GOALS

(SMART: specific, measurable, achievable, relevant, time-constrained)

SMART, Positively-framed LONG-term Goal:

Achieve, Fix, resolve, stop, eliminate (example: "I want to focus my sexual energy completely (100%) toward my partner for the rest of my life, as evidenced by redirecting an urge for porn into a bid for connection with my partner.")

SMART, Positively-framed <u>SHORT</u>-term Goal:

Increase, improve, reduce, relieve (example: "I will increase my self-awareness when triggered to view porn; every morning and acutely as needed I will look at the feelings wheel to identify all present emotions while also observing any self-talk, core beliefs showing up so as to increase my emotional awareness and document these findings.")

∽

Again, and in closing, you ultimately want to establish the Long-Term (LT) Goal and then break it down into Short-Term (ST) Goals, positively framed and utilizing a SMART goal framework.

Later, we'll be further breaking down the concept of 'Process' vs. 'Outcome' and it's application in how to most effectively achieve sustainability. Simply put, an outcome is determined by your process - but...

- How do you measure that?
- WHO gets to define success?
- How often will you check-in with your success measurement?
- Lastly, how will you know if you're going off the rails.

PRIMARY PRESENTING "PROBLEM"
YOUR BEHAVIOR MAKES SENSE...
OR ELSE YOU'RE NONSENSICAL.

PRIMARY PRESENTING PROBLEMS

A PRIMARY PRESENTING PROBLEM IS THE INITIAL ISSUE OR SYMPTOM THAT CAUSES A person to seek recovery from their addiction. In a medical sense, your primary presenting problem would answer the doctor's question, "What are you in for today?" It's important to fully understand your own problem in order to solve it. This means acknowledging the problem's origins, reflecting back on how it started, when you first recognized it as a "problem," and what it took for that recognition to take place. While reflecting, it helps to recall the emotions felt at different points in the development of your problem.

Strong emotions have the ability to both enhance and impair long-term memory retention. Emotions like anger, excitement, and fear "wake you up" and streamline your attention to important stimuli. Thinking back to times you've felt these "alert" emotions can direct you to significant moments of your journey. On the other side of this coin, excess stress, depression, and sickness are all likely to impair cognitive function, affecting the brain's memory retention process. So, perceived "gaps" in your memory can also act as clues to important moments.

Think about the very first time you thought, "I might have a problem," consciously or otherwise— and go from there. When did you first feel the urge to fix it? What were the efforts you made to do so? Were any of these efforts successful, even slightly so?

By looking back on your failures and successes, you equip yourself with the knowledge of what works and what doesn't. The following exercise allows for reflection on your problem and what it means to you.

What Is Your Primary Presenting Problem?

When did you first recognize you had a problem?

Have you ever successfully stopped? For how long?

How has or has not the problem escalated?

Have you noticed anything new while reflecting on your problem?

3

BECOMING A SELF-EXPERT
SOBRIETY IS CHEAP. SUSTAINABILITY IS EVERYTHING.

Perhaps the most vital tool to possess as you continue your journey towards sustainable sexual integrity is **self-expertise**. From here on out, we want to shift away from the perspective that there is a "problem" to be "stopped." It's not about quitting a behavior. Rather, it's about becoming an expert on yourself. In order to do this, you need to understand how this problematic behavior made sense to you, even at one point in time. What **need** was this behavior solving? In a sense, your behavior acted as a solution. The big question for you to determine is what that solution was for.

Sustainable sexual integrity is founded in an understanding of the self. By understanding the emotions, wants, and needs inside of you, you begin facing the issue with presence and awareness, rather than white-knuckling your way through the day, fighting the urge to do the things you "shouldn't" do. Though simple-seeming, this shift in mindset is challenging for men, in particular. Typically, men aren't taught to understand or reflect on their deeper emotions. Because of this, it's difficult to identify and reconcile complicated feelings of shame, abandonment, inadequacy, and worthlessness.

It's easy to recognize surface-level emotions and needs. You recognize angry. You recognize hungry. You recognize horny. You *know* how to meet these needs. It's important to be able to process deeper emotions in the same way. Now, it's time to move in the direction of self-expertise. You'll work to reframe your struggle and identify the specific, valid emotions that drive your behavior. A daily check-in is a wonderful way to start exercising the muscles of self-awareness and self-regulation. Engaging daily with your sobriety increases your presence, reinforcing the connection between you and your internal processes.

Next, I will walk you through what a daily, or regular, check-in could look like. Allow me to encourage you strongly to only stick with the items in the check-in that you find valuable. You do not need to do all the components, and feel free to add your own. Your check-in, ideally is something that you're looking forward to doing - not a chore.

THE DAILY CHECK-IN EXERCISE

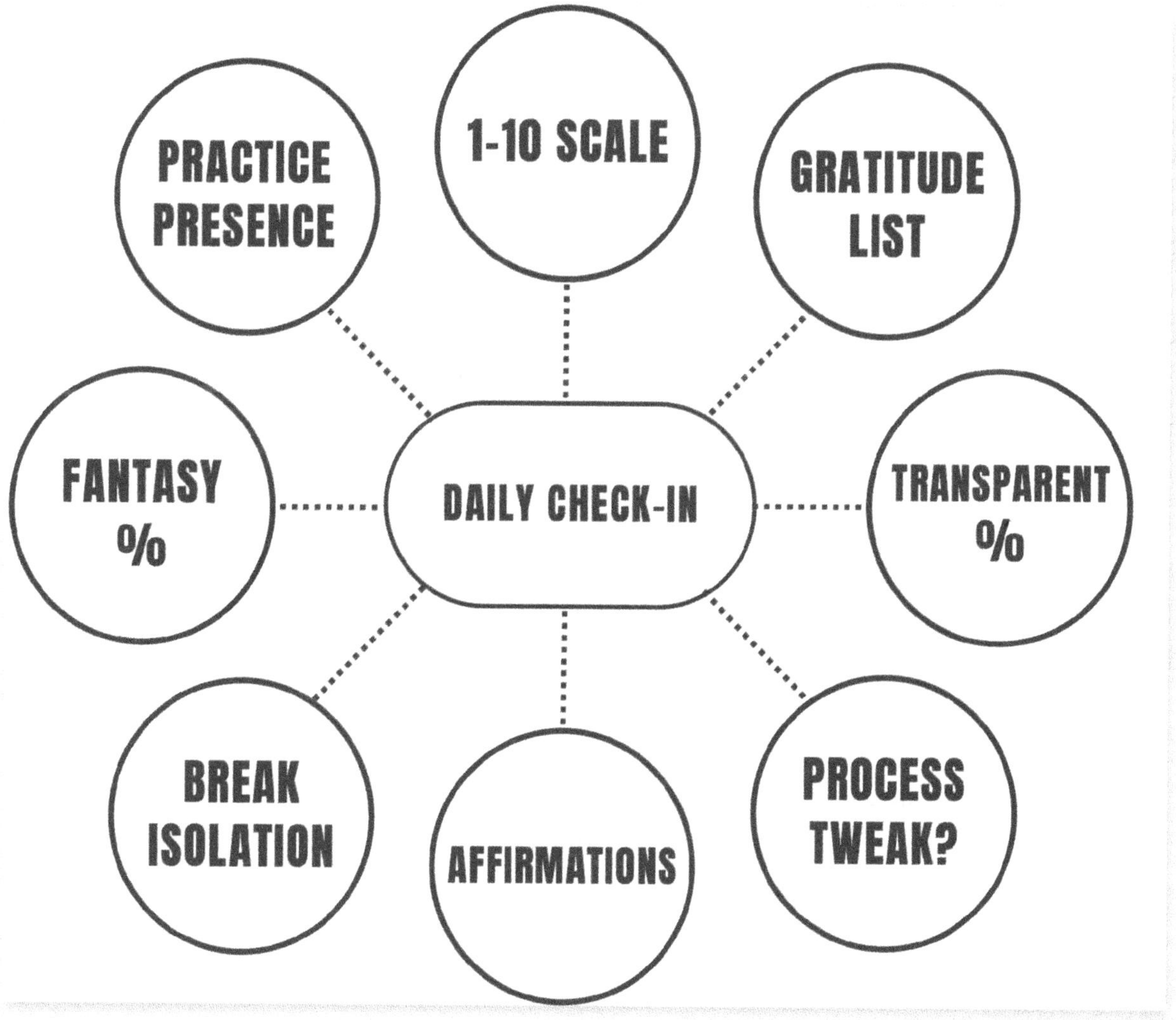

DAILY CHECK-IN

DAILY CHECK-IN

1-10 Scale

Every evening, determine "how you're doing" on a scale of 1-10 (10 being the best day of your life, 1 being the worst). If today, you're at a 7, think about what it would take for that number to be an 8, or a 9. What would elevate your day by one or two points? Then, ask yourself, what's preventing you from being at a 6? Now, let's say you're at a 3. What's stopping you from plummeting to a 1? Understanding these minor differences is essential to your growth. This information helps to make your good days better, and your bad days less bad. Lastly, try and think back to your last five "10" days. Try and identify any common threads between them.

Gratitude List

Take a moment to write down five things you feel grateful for. It can be big or small, the same five every day or wildly different, anything you'd like. The idea is to keep the things we're grateful for present in our minds. If you find yourself struggling with this one, go back to basics: food, water, shelter, etc.

Transparent %

Think back on the last 24 hours. What percentage of those 24 hours would you say were lived in full transparency? No secrets, no deception, no compartmentalization of your compulsive behavior. Count your waking hours.

Process Tweak

You never wanna be caught looking at the scoreboard. Approach your behavior one play at a time, one pitch at a time. Once you're able to do so, you've successfully developed your own process of handling yourself, your life, and your addiction. That said— no process is perfect. Take a moment to think on the last 24 hours. Were there any moments of frustration? Triggers? Cravings? Acting out? Which part of your process broke down? Maybe part of your process works great on Tuesday afternoons but falls apart on a Friday night. Each day, try to identify points in your process that could benefit from adjustment.

Affirmations

Oftentimes, our past is filled with shame, regret, and perceived failures. These emotions can be devastating for our self-concept. Try implementing three affirmations to voice aloud during your daily check-in. These can be anything you like. Some examples: "I have value." / "I'm not who I want to be, but I'm not who I used to be." / "All anyone has is today, so today I will do the things I know are healthiest for me."

Break Isolation

Problematic sexual behavior thrives in isolation. Breaking isolation can break the behavior. This could look like calling a friend, attending a support group, or simply going to the grocery store. Get up, get dressed, and get out. At this point of your check-in, ask yourself, "How am I going to break isolation today?"

Fantasy %

The first stage of the addiction cycle is preoccupation, or fantasizing. This means you've been triggered by something and are craving relief or satisfaction. Here, you reach the gate of the addiction cycle, which presents two choices: an attempt at healthy relief, or an entrance into the addiction cycle. To avoid the preoccupation stage, it's important to stay present and aware of triggers as they occur and choose to leverage interventions for a healthier outcome. So, take a moment to think about the last 24 hours and ask yourself, "What percentage of the last 24 hours did I spend preoccupied or fantasizing?"

Practice Presence

As you round out your daily check-in, take a moment to just be present. Ultimately, the present moment is all we have. In his book, "The Power of Now," Eckart Tolle says, "Realize deeply that the present moment is all you have. Make the NOW the primary focus of your life." Practicing presence is a muscle that you will begin to flex and understand within yourself. This can look like setting an intention for the day while drinking your morning coffee, completing a guided meditation, taking some time to journal, or simply walking your dog.

∼

Daily check-in pages found in the back of the book

RELAPSE PREVENTION PLAN
IT IS IMPOSSIBLE TO HATE YOURSELF INTO HEALTHY

RELAPSE PREVENTION

While not a requirement, relapse is a common part of the recovery process for many people. Relapse is not something to be feared. Rather, it's important to be knowledgeable and prepared for possible missteps on your path to recovery. The process of relapsing can be isolating and discouraging, leading many to believe they have "failed" themselves or others (Abstinence Violation Effect).

Instead of punishing yourself, work to validate the pattern, understand as much as you possibly can, apply your addiction cycle (Chapter 4) learnings and prepare a new intervention for next time. Slip ups, relapses are simply data points along a continuum that's been in motion likely for decades. Problematic patterns weren't developed overnight and won't be rid over night. If one truly wants to achieve a healthier space - higher group - then they must appreciate that the thing is not the thing and seek to best understand how 'acting out' made sense in a given moment. If this cannot be achieved then one will be left with the untenable notion that they simply don't make sense at times, which is a position that is impossible to break from.

It is impossible to hate yourself into healthy.

Accept where you are at, learn from it as best you are able and commit a path ahead - preferably aligned with your values.

Your path toward sustainable sexual sobriety from problematic sexual behavior will be defined by either **presence** or **absence** - I guarantee it. Someone with a sexual sobriety defined by absence may not be acting on their impulses, but still find themselves consumed by thoughts of the behaviors they are actively trying not to engage with. This person might obsessively count the days of their sobriety, wake up conscious of what they shouldn't do, or fear their possibility of relapse.

An individual with a sexual sobriety defined by **presence** is engaged and intentional with their life and how they fill their days. They are empowered by a life separate from addiction. They experience occasional triggers and cravings, but their focus remains on the fulfillment they receive from life.

Relapse means something different to everyone. In this next exercise, the three circles, you will be rewarded with clarity of mind and process as you work to pinpoint your own definition of relapse, understanding of your personal triggers, and identifying the ways in which you fill your own life with meaning. A clear-cut and unambiguous relapse prevention plan is one of your most powerful tools in sustaining sexual sobriety.

4

YOUR RELAPSE PREVENTION PLAN

SECTION 1

Self-Expert Assessment

How did you come to engage in this problematic behavior?

_____

_____

_____

When did you recognize it as problematic?

_____

_____

_____

SECTION 1

Self-Expert Assessment

What negative consequences have resulted?

_____

_____

_____

Why did you remain stuck in this pattern?

_____

_____

_____

How can you be CONFIDENT (not hopeful) that your future will differ from your past?

_____

_____

_____

What new tools, insights, or awareness have you acquired recently?

_____

_____

_____

SECTION 2

Identification of Triggers

Internal Triggers (thoughts, emotions, sensations):

→ _____

→ _____

→ _____

→ _____

→ _____

External Triggers (people, places, situations):

→ _____

→ _____

→ _____

→ _____

→ _____

SECTION 3

Early Warning Signs

Behavioral Signs:

→ _____

→ _____

→ _____

Emotional Signs:

→ _____

→ _____

→ _____

Cognitive Signs (thought patterns):

→ _____

→ _____

→ _____

SECTION 4

Coping Strategies

Immediate Coping Techniques (actions to take immediately when triggered):

→ _____

→ _____

→ _____

→ _____

→ _____

Long-term Coping Skills (ongoing practices to manage stress and maintain wellness):

→ _____

→ _____

→ _____

→ _____

→ _____

SECTION 5

The Three Circles Exercise (graphic on page 9)

Inner Circle (behaviors to avoid entirely):

→ _____

→ _____

→ _____

Middle Circle (behaviors requiring caution):

→ _____

→ _____

→ _____

Outer Circle (healthy behaviors encouraged):

→ _____

→ _____

→ _____

SECTION 6

Defense Mechanisms and Rationalizations

Historical Defense Mechanisms (preferred):

→ _____

→ _____

→ _____

→ _____

→ _____

Problematic Future Defense Mechanisms:

→ _____

→ _____

→ _____

→ _____

→ _____

SECTION 7

Bounce Back Plan (if relapse occurs)

Steps to Immediately Regain Control and Recover:

1. _____

2. _____

3. _____

4. _____

5. _____

SECTION 8

The Feelings Component

Identify Your SINGLE Most Difficult Emotion (The Boogeyman Emotion):

_____

_____

_____

_____

_____

∾

SECTION 9

Support System

Personal Support Contacts:

Name: _____

Phone: _____

-

Name: _____

Phone: _____

-

Name: _____

Phone: _____

-

Professional Support Contacts:

Therapist/Counselor: _____

Phone: _____

-

Peer Support: _____

Phone: _____

SECTION 10

Crisis Plan

Steps to Follow in Case of Relapse Risk or Crisis:

1. _____

2. _____

3. _____

4. _____

Emergency Contacts:

Crisis Line: _____

Emergency Services (911)

SECTION 11

Plan Sharing and Assessment

Who will you share this plan with?

Name: _____

Relationship: _____

Assessment Frequency: how often will you revisit and update this plan?

_____

_____

SECTION 12

Comprehensive Reflection Questions

Why am I committed to change now?

_____

_____

_____

What is my biggest motivation to stay sober/healthy?

_____

_____

_____

Which coping skill has been most effective so far?

_____

_____

_____

Which coping skill have I avoided using and why?

_____

_____

_____

How can I leverage my personal strengths?

_____

_____

How can my support system better assist me?

Which triggers remain the most challenging?

What are the proactive measures I will implement immediately?

What negative thoughts often precede relapse behaviors?

What have past relapses taught me?

_____

_____

How can I better identify early relapse signs?

_____

_____

_____

What healthy alternatives will replace my problematic behaviors?

_____

_____

_____

Who holds me accountable?

_____

_____

_____

How will I manage intense cravings or urges?

_____

_____

_____

What emotional needs did my problematic behavior fulfill?

YOUR RELAPSE PREVENTION PLAN

How will I meet these emotional needs differently now?

Which rationalizations are hardest to resist?

How will I respond differently when rationalizations arise?

What daily habits contribute to my wellness?

How will I track my emotional well-being?

_____

_____

_____

What specific actions will I take during high-risk situations?

_____

_____

_____

What are my self-care priorities?

_____

_____

_____

How will I rebuild trust with loved ones affected by past behaviors?

_____

_____

_____

How will I celebrate progress and milestones?

_____

_____

What new understanding about myself is critical for sustained recovery?

_____

_____

_____

∼

Commitment Statement

I, _____, commit to implementing this relapse prevention plan. I understand my triggers and warning signs, and I agree to use my coping strategies and proactively reach out to my support system.

Signature: _____ Date: _____

THE THREE CIRCLES EXERCISE
INNER, MIDDLE & OUTER CIRCLES

∼

The three circles is a required exercise in striving for sustainable sexual integrity. In contemplating and executing on the three circles you will bring clarity, remove or relieve ambiguity and focus your direction on presence and purpose, not absence in your life. This exercise can be incredibly helpful to share with partners as well, limiting future confusion as to what is 'in bounds' and what is 'out of bounds' as the three circles brings forth clarity in these areas.

It is incredibly common to see the lack of clarity in the areas of the three circles when relapse has occurred, which is why I'd recommend prioritizing this effort and returning to it and least monthly within your first year.

Lastly, remember that your three circles are living venues, they are always changing, so it should be considered how often you will return to update your three circles. I would propose weekly at first and then moving to monthly as is appropriate for you.

∼

THREE CIRCLES EXERCISE
RELAPSE PREVENTION PLANNING

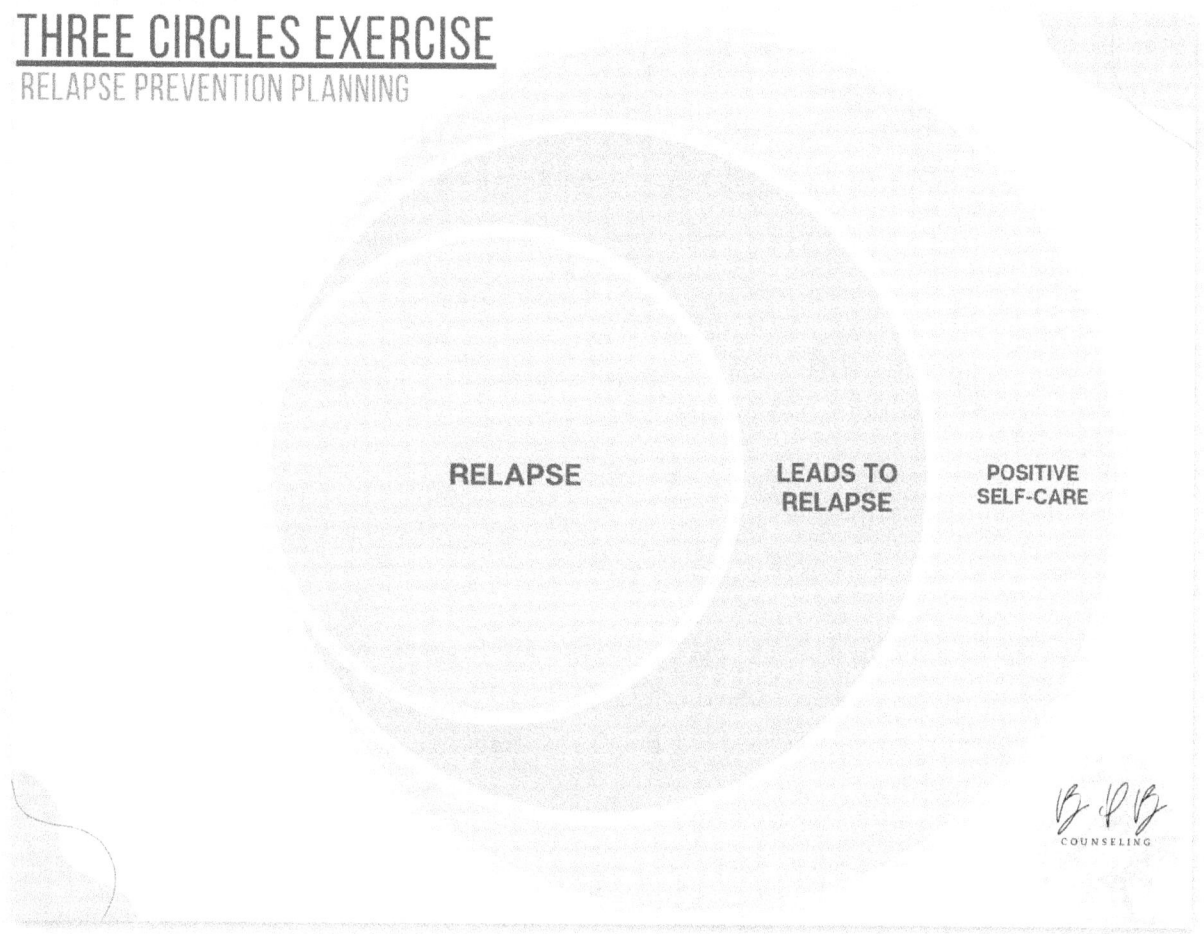

RELAPSE

Clearly outline all behaviors that meet your definition of relapse. Be as exhaustive and specific as possible.

LEADS TO RELAPSE

Outline behaviors, triggers, scenarios, events, people, places, music, substances, venues, seasons, times of day, and emotions that increase your likelihood of relapse.

POSITIVE SELF-CARE

Define your sexual sobriety with presence. Outline activities, relationships, passions, and hobbies that bring you joy and fill up your life. This can act as a list of gratitude for the things you already have, or a list of things you want to implement into your life. They can be big or small, as long as it brings meaning to you.

THREE CIRCLES EXERCISE

INNER CIRCLE: RELAPSE. What is your definition of Relapse, what are absolute no-go, third-rail behaviors for you (inner circle)... e.g. watching porn, messaging others, etc.

_____

_____

_____

_____

MIDDLE CIRCLE: LEADS TO RELAPSE. Middle circle behaviors are not relapse, in and of themselves, but they are actions that SOMETIMES, are more likely to lead you in the direction of acting out (middle circle)... e.g. doom scrolling social media, alcohol, etc.

_____

_____

_____

_____

OUTER CIRCLE: Purpose, Meaning, Passion and/or Positive self-care (outer circle)... e.g. exercise, meditation, building community, helping others, pursuing a degree/promotion, etc.

_____

_____

_____

_____

5

FEELINGS, CONSEQUENCES, HISTORY & PATHOLOGY

EMOTIONAL REGULATION

CHECKING IN DAILY IS ESSENTIAL TO STAYING IN TUNE WITH YOUR PROGRESS AND emotions. But how do we identify these deeper, more complicated feelings as they arise? A wheel of emotions is another tool to reference at any point in your recovery or daily life. The concept of an emotion wheel was first brought about by American psychologist Dr. Robert Plutchik, who proposed that all complex feelings can be traced back to a small number of primary emotions. This idea was then developed by Dr. Gloria Willcox and named The Feelings Wheel.

You cannot solve a problem without first identifying it.

I dare say that you cannot even improve a problem without first identifying it.

If you cannot identify what it is that is going on inside you, then I'd propose you may be trying to answer a question that is not being asked. Even if you discovered the "right" answer, it's misapplied to the wrong question.

It's easier to understand, assess and as needed begin to address these big emotions when we can take a beat, put a name to them, and process accordingly. This tool allows you to expand your emotional vocabulary and regulate your emotions in a healthier, more effective manner. On page 16 is a wheel of emotions for you to utilize, reference, and depend on as you continue your recovery.

At the center of the wheel, you'll find seven basic emotions. Sit with how you feel for a moment. Pick a core emotion, then work your way outwards to the second and third tiers. Examine the emotions until you land on one that feels true to you at this moment. A crucial step in overcoming compulsive sexual behavior is learning to make room for emotion. Your instinct may be to resist your negative feelings. But true healing lies in the ability to embrace your emotions—especially the heavy, painful ones. The tool here is "staying with", can you stay with or share the room with your difficult emotions.

Imagine you're wading in the ocean, and each wave is an emotion. As a wave begins to form, rising before you like a big, blue wall, your instincts demand you retreat back to shore. But, as you run from the wave, it crashes into you with great force and wraps you up in it's current, rendering you powerless. Instead of fleeing your feelings: lean into them. Swim up to the wave. Ride out each wave of emotion as they rise and fall, following the current without judgment or resistance.

One last piece of advice as you venture into the feelings wheel. Identify as many emotions as you possibly can in the moment. It's perfectly normal to identify 15-30 different emotions existing inside of you at any given moment. This is super important. Often times it is not that you are feeling one incredibly difficult emotion, but rather it is that you are experiencing 25 different difficult emotions simultaneously. The sheer volume of emotions can sometimes be enough to trigger, regardless of which emotions are present. Consider this as a possibility in your efforts to understand all that is going on inside of you.

FEELINGS, CONSEQUENCES, HISTORY & PATHOLOGY

45

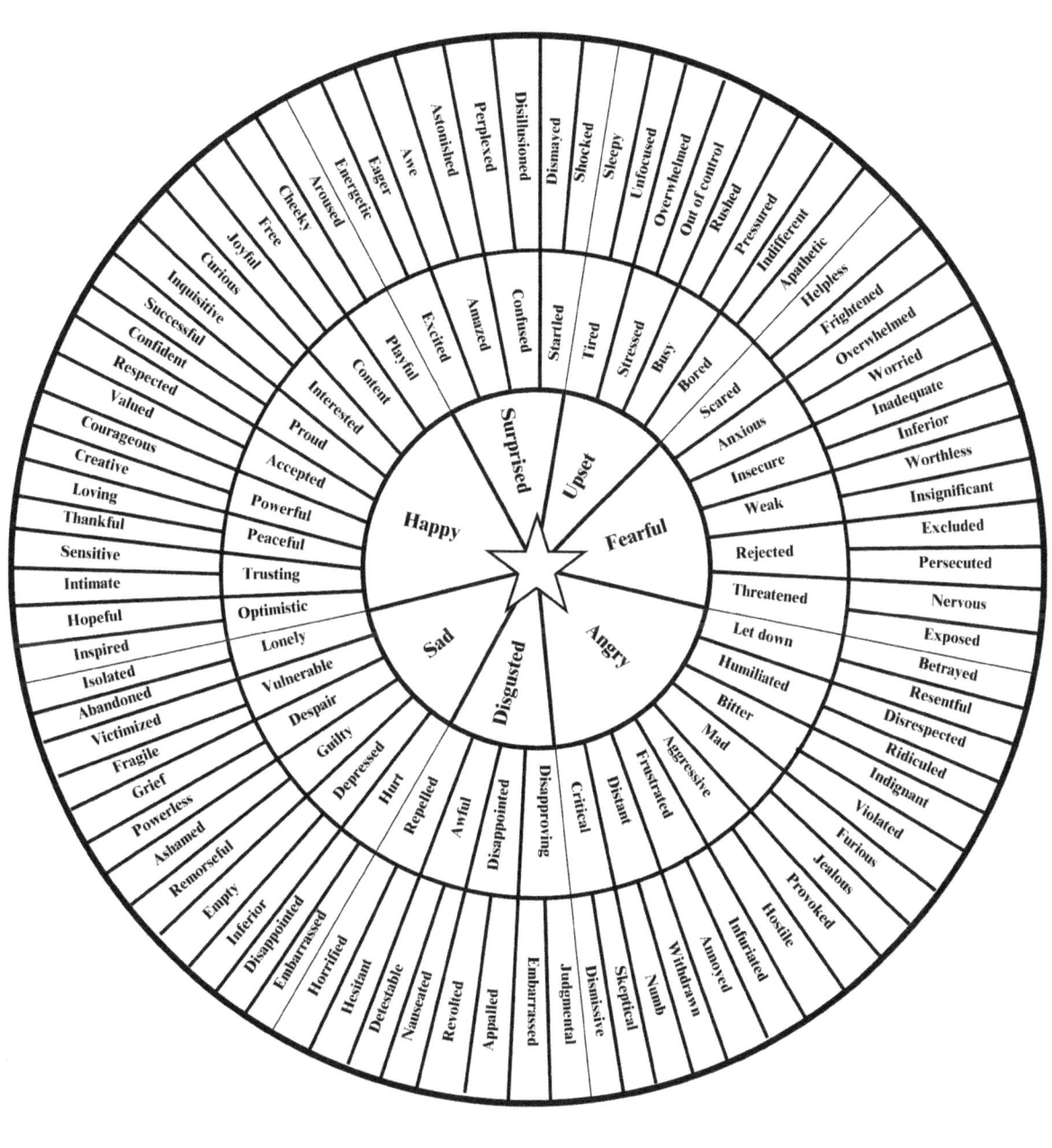

BEHAVIORAL INVENTORY

By now you have successfully identified the primary presenting problem, established some short and long-term goals, and are growing in this new muscle of self-expertise.

Next, let's take an inventory of the problem for the purpose of further understanding and growth. For this exercise, you'll spend some time reflecting on and answering prompts designed to help you observe and assess yourself from a variety of angles. Be as exhaustive and specific as possible.

How long has this behavior been a problem?

_____

_____

_____

_____

_____

Has this behavior been escalating, plateaued or getting better?

_____

_____

_____

_____

_____

What exactly *are* these behaviors? Porn? Infidelity? Name them.

Have I ever been able to successfully stop the behavior before?

How did I first *know* this behavior is a problem?

_____

_____

Who is this behavior a problem to? My partner? My family? Me?

_____

_____

_____

_____

What makes this problem a big deal? Why do I want to fix it?

_____

_____

_____

_____

∾

NEGATIVE CONSEQUENCE INVENTORY

Next, you'll take an inventory of the negative consequences brought forth by your problem. Think of all the ways in which you, your partner, your job, your social life, your finances, etc. have been negatively impacted by your problematic behavior. List as many instances and examples you can think of. In the future, continue coming back to this every 90 days to see if your understanding of negative consequences has changed.

Negative Consequence Inventory

SEXUAL HISTORY INVENTORY

This next inventory is intended to help you map out the history of your sexual behavior problem. Some people prefer to create this inventory as a timeline, but general notes work just as well. Go back in time to when the problem first started, and work forward from there. Effectively you want to document moments and/or patterns of acting out where negative consequences surfaced or there were violation of your values or identity.

Sexual History Inventory

THE RECOVERY TIMELINE

THERE ARE MANY IDEAS ABOUT WHAT THE TYPICAL "RECOVERY TIMELINE" LOOKS LIKE for problematic sexual behavior. The most commonly held belief is that the timeline for recovery spans roughly five years, suggesting it takes five years for an individual to reach a healthy, well-adjusted position. In my experience, this is generally not the case. So, here, I'm going to highlight the variables I most often see with individuals who are able to achieve recovery in a much shorter time frame.

There is a distinct correlation between the severity of **negative consequences** and the length of recovery. To put it simply, when someone's life is entirely out of control (unable to maintain self-imposed boundaries, experiencing damage to their finances, relationships, sense of self-worth), they will face a significantly longer recovery timeline. In comparison, a person who is largely able to manage their problematic behavior will find themselves on a much shorter recovery timeline. This person may experience a loss of control, but is able to return to a healthier position for a significant amount of time. Additionally, the negative consequences, though present, are less devastating.

Another factor in the length of your recovery is your **immediate primary support structure**. Most often, this is your family. Was your partner impacted by your problematic behavior? Your kids? The impact on these relationships, and the dynamics within them, needs to be understood. Once understood, the work must be done to begin healing. So, the number of relationships that require attention will add time to your recovery as well.

It's important to find and appreciate the beauty, joy, and celebration within and along your recovery journey as a whole. Be careful not to fall into the trap of, "When I reach the end of my recovery timeline, I'll finally be happy." By delaying your own happiness to some abstract point in time, you effectively remove any ability to achieve said happiness in the present moment. Finding contentment within your recovery is crucial to success. It may sound difficult—if it were easy, everyone would be doing it. But ultimately, the ability to celebrate yourself and find satisfaction along the recovery timeline is an integral part of your sustainability.

The goal is not to navigate the recovery timeline perfectly, but to navigate it **simply**. Above all, ask yourself, "How do I stay on the path?" You must find a way to stay on the path when things are good, when things are difficult, when things are sideways, and when things don't make sense. This perseverance is most important. On the following page, you'll find the typical stages of the recovery timeline: crisis/decision, shock, grief, healing, and growth.

THE RECOVERY TIMELINE

1. CRISIS/DECISION
Negative consequences have caught up. It's time to decide if you're going to get help or unravel further.

2. SHOCK
Realizing your personal/relational/life expectations have not been met. The results of your negative consequences are staring you in the face.

3. GRIEF
Denial, anger, bargaining, depression, acceptance. You grieve the death of your friend, the addiction. You grieve the life you thought you had.

4. REPAIR
You've committed to recovery, processed the death of what was, and are beginning to repair what's been broken in your warpath.

5. GROWTH
The harsh winter and spring showers are over. Now it's time to blossom.

∼

Typical recovery, similar for both yourself and your partner, shows up in roughly five major ways, and while I'm representing them here as somewhat linear, each and any of the five stages can and will show up at any time along the continuum.

Crisis is where it all begins. This is where discovery typically happens. Here, primarily everyone is assessing immediate remediation - should I stay or go. At this point, considerable shock and grief have already begun presenting themselves, however, they are not predominant yet, as the 'fog of war' has not settled. Additionally worth noting that growth and repair has actually begun in some fashion and to a small degree, yet it has begun.

Shock typically enters next. The shock of what each party believed about the relationship itself, the shock about what the betrayed partner believed about you - who you are, values, identity, etc. Again, the crisis is still present, but the dust from initial discovery/confrontation has settled more into shock.

Grief comes next, mostly grief around the loss of a relationship - even if the couple stays together it is not the same relationship (albeit the potential for a stronger relationship is out there to be had, yet it'll still be different). There is grief over expectations; of holidays, of closeness, of weddings, funerals, birthdays, vacations, etc. Often times for you there is a grieving process for the addiction itself as the addiction has become a romantic and supportive partner in many ways as it was always present and available when called upon. The loss of this ever-present and effective 'partner' is a grieving process in its own right and it's in this stage and beyond when 'euphoric recall' can play a part. This is when one recalls 'the good old days', the brain will smooth off rough edges and recollection of the finer times will return, often leaving out the painful memories.

Repair is next. Repair has begun since the beginning, but with time, consistency, transparency, reliability and tons of new information presented by way of learnings, insights, vulnerability, transparency repair may continue it's work and start to take hold.

Growth is the final stage worth noting. Now, of course growth has been ongoing the entire time, yet in this stage it really begins to shine through and dominate the stage. Both parties have worked to understand, introspect, discover safety within themselves and establish safe vulnerability in their relationship which has given way to incredible growth.

6

PROCESS

THE BIGGEST LITTLE WORD IN BEHAVIOR CHANGE

Process is one of the most substantive components of your relapse prevention plan. In this chapter, you'll learn to understand the nature of process and gain the ability to document your own. Process, at its core, is any action that helps you move in a healthier direction. Some also refer to this as "program," but for this stage of your recovery, it's helpful to examine process with one question in mind: "What can I do to move in a healthier direction?" For our purposes, think of process in this way:

Process = Intentional action - preventative and acute - moving one in a healthier direction.

First and foremost, if you do not have a documented process, you do not have a process. Often, people begin moving in healthier directions, reestablishing trust in their relationships, and achieving their desired outcomes, but find themselves unable to explain **how** all of this happened.

They achieve success but are unable to show their math, so to speak.

If a path to success cannot be expressed or taught at an expert level, then the path may as well be credited to happenstance or luck and thus unable to be replicated. Documenting process - both preventative and acute - will provide the underlying structure enabling iterative progress with significantly less turmoil, wasted effort and tension.

Your highest priority in this chapter is to understand and then document your process. Write it down. Capture it on page.

WHY IS PROCESS IMPORTANT?

It's imperative to understand how to begin moving in a healthier direction. Notice in my writing the absence of words like "right", "better", or "good" when referring to this movement with one's self. Instead I will most often use "healthy" and this is with great intention.

Qualifiers such as right, better or good are often relative and originate from an extrinsic variable or a source outside of yourself. If you ask a room of 10 people, "What is right? What is good? What is better?" You are likely to receive 20 different answers for . If you ask the same group of 10 to define something as healthy or unhealthy, generally, the group will find it easier to come to a consensus.

So, as we work, let's attempt to remove all third-party voices and focus on what is healthy for you (self-efficacy). Some people, as they begin their journey toward sexual sobriety, feel that they need to abstain from any kind of sexual behavior whatsoever. This would include masturbation, intimacy with their partner, etc. Who's to say whether or not this path is "right" or "better" for you - the pope, your spouse, your mom, your therapist, the Dalai Lama?? What about younger you - certainly younger you and present-day you would not be in full agreement on the definition of right.

I'm not a fan of 'better' as better subtly hints - or not so subtly - that before today, I was 'worse.' While I understand that one may view their patterns of behavior as remorseful, dysfunctional, destructive, betrayal, often times this perspective that "I'm better than today than I was before" leaves one carrying a largely self-critical position of themselves - just of their slightly younger self.

This self-critical view will bring with it significant tension which your brain and body will desperately seek a path out from under. I believe there is a sweet spot where one can avoid blame shifting, avoid personalization (graphic below), and live in a place of healthy accountability.

In *humanistic (experiential/person-centered)* approaches the central mechanism of change in work with the inner critic transforms the disruptive process into a more adaptive self-aspect that forms part of the flexible and dynamic self-process. The inner critic can be transformed through the change processes. Researchers conclude that in the *client-centered/experiential literature* there are three well-known ways of achieving a fluid and complex self-organization: removing the experiential block, restoring interactions between various self-aspects and developing an active and integral "I". Each of these draws on the belief that the "inner critic needs to be approached in an active way, as it will not change or disappear of its own accord".

ŠOKOVÁ, B., GREŠKOVIČOVÁ, K., HALAMOVÁ, J., & BARÁNKOVÁ, M. (2025)

A Framework to avoid dysfunctional self-critical thinking:

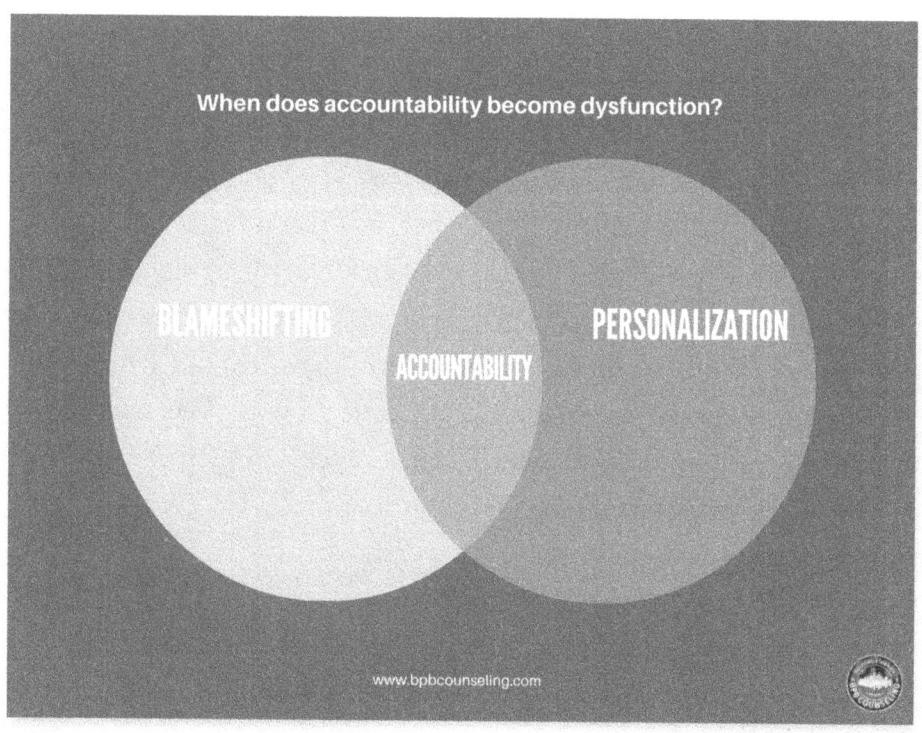

Own what's yours to own - and only that.

To determine what is healthy, one must start by establishing standards. Consider your idea of "healthy." What behaviors would manifest a **healthy ideal** for me?

From there, how would I define **success**? By process, or outcome? Intrinsic or extrinsic? How often would I like to come back and assess whether or not the path I'm on is leading me in a healthier direction?

Let's use an example:

> I WANT TO BE A BETTER SPOUSE.

What are the behaviors that would prove this to your spouse... the world... yourself?

> I CAN PLAN A WEEKLY DATE-NIGHT, A WEEKLY SIT-DOWN "STATE OF THE UNION" CONVERSATION ABOUT OUR RELATIONSHIP (SEPARATE FROM DATE-NIGHT), MAKE DAILY BIDS FOR AFFECTION, REGULARLY CHECK-IN AND ASK HOW MY PARTNER IS DOING AND PROACTIVELY CONSIDER THEM AS I GO ABOUT MY DAY. I BELIEVE ALL OF THESE ACTIONS WILL BRING ME CLOSER TO MY "HEALTHY IDEAL" (BEING A BETTER SPOUSE).

Notice that these behaviors are more **process** than outcomes.

Additionally, these behaviors are positively framed. They're telling me what you WILL be doing, not what you WON'T be doing.

So, as you construct your success metric, you want to set your standards definitively and comprehensively. Many individuals make great progress, but find themselves without a clear way to document or measure where they begin, where they are, and where they want to go. Recording your progress allows you to appreciate your growth. The success metric is not a carrot to dangle in front of your face, or some image of success to keep you motivated. Rather, it is often a way to recognize progress and celebrate yourself. Of course, it also serves as a measuring stick for where you are and where you want to be.

Oftentimes with the success metric, an individual achieves their goals and finds them to be different than what they imagined. This is partly human nature—we decide, "Once I get this house, or this job, or this partner, or have kids, or get the kids off to college, or become a millionaire, then, I'll finally be happy." It's only natural to think like this. But, of course, some people achieve all of these things. Some of them are happy, and some of them are not. So, direct the question back to yourself. How do I identify my level of progress in the direction healthiest for me? Let's go back to the example:

> AM I DOING 100% OF WHAT I SAID I'D DO (TO BECOME A BETTER SPOUSE) 100% OF THE TIME? OR RATHER, IS MY GOAL TO ACHIEVE 70% OF THOSE BEHAVIORS FIVE DAYS A WEEK?

~

Another way to approach this is by using an outcome metric, however, be aware the difference between intrinsic and extrinsic outcomes measures.

Example - Extrinsic Outcome:

> I'VE BEEN TRYING TO BECOME A BETTER SPOUSE IN MANY DIFFERENT WAYS. DOES MY PARTNER BELIEVE I'M SUCCEEDING IN BECOMING A BETTER SPOUSE?

This example is an **extrinsic outcome metric**. Extrinsic metrics can be risky because they exist outside of your control. Outcome metrics can be risky as well, because there are often many variables throughout the process that can impact the outcome despite your best effort and intent. It is highly likely that the 'undoing' defense mechanism may lead you to not even believing that your own assessment of yourself is worthwhile. This will lead to a dangerous cycle for both you and your partner where the warden/prisoner dynamic is likely to play out, you will feel completely disempowered and your partner - while garnering a sense of control - will now be carrying the burden of your emotional/self-worth stability.

You do also have the option to establish intrinsic outcome metrics to assess your progress and success. This could look like:

> I SUCCEEDED AT BEING FULLY TRANSPARENT THIS WEEK
> I DID NOT ACT OUT AT ALL THIS WEEK

These are clearly defined outcomes that are largely within your purview.

Having said that, I would highly recommend an **intrinsic process metric** as the best method of evaluation. The more that you're able to engage and operate in an aware, informed, authentic and empowered position, the more likely sobriety will be. Focusing on both what is within your locus of control (*intrinsic*) and what single movement can you make today to move in a direction MOST LIKELY to achieve your desired outcome (*process*) - both being in your control - this is much more likely to get you where you want to be long term.

The big, big thing to keep in mind here: "Am I moving in a healthier direction?"

This is all one big process. It's important to understand and appreciate this as a process. Think left foot, right foot, left foot, right foot, etc. You don't know what you don't know, and your process may change as you progress and gain new information about yourself. Very likely the very outcome you've been chasing after will change as you stay engaged in your process. Certainly your definition of what's "healthy" for you will continue to evolve over time as well as your idea of what's possible will evolve. Due to these changing variables - sometimes wildly -

this is why assessment becomes such a critical piece in ensuring that you're staying on track or becoming aware as you're moving off-track. In assessing whether or not one is moving in a healthier direction, there must be a point in time to pause and reflect on the progress made, despite your brain's desire to keep moving ahead and onward to the next threat.

Without this moment of reflection, you may miss the chance to celebrate your growth and acknowledge the strides you've made. Though this acknowledgment seems simple, it plays an important role in your motivation to recover. Often, people can become discouraged along the path to recovery, feeling guilt and shame about their progress, wishing they were doing "better." This negative outlook can incite a cycle of inadequate feelings, but it can be deterred with a commitment to appreciating progress (no matter how small).

Assessment is also an incredible opportunity to reevaluate your healthy ideals. Maybe you've come close to your goal, or even achieved it, but the outcome isn't what you thought it would be. Rather than a setback, this is an opportunity to take stock and possibly change what "healthy" looks like for you.

(Possibly) my favorite part of the assessment phase is the **safety net**. When an individual knows there's an assessment on the schedule, even if it's a month from now, it allows them to move forward in all possible pathways with confidence, or, dare I say, beautiful recklessness. They are not afraid of failure. They might even be seeking out failure, to learn from it. Because of the "safety net" that occurs every 30 days, the assessment often empowers individuals to engage with their recovery in new and exciting ways.

One note on partners. It is often incredibly difficult for a betrayed partner to see the very person who has hurt them the most start to do incredibly well and becoming healthier. The undoing defense mechanisms will often activate inside of you, telling you to stop making progress, or don't show it, hide your optimism, hope, healing as it is difficult for your partner to see.

I would propose that both can exist simultaneously. I would propose that...

_____

With a healthy YOU, all boats rise.

_____

This is an incredibly difficult and painful process, yet as you're beginning to see, understand and achieve things within yourself that you never even considered were possible, allow yourself to lean into your own healing AND engage with your partner with the utmost empathy, curiosity, patience and kindness.

Before we start documenting your process: let's talk about the brain. The brain's sole concern is **efficient survival**. It does not want to pause and reflect on the past, it wants to look forward—to scan for threats to your survival. I believe this is why the reflection and assessment phase is often overlooked in recovery work. In recovery, we are always moving to the next burning platform, the next challenge, the next threat. Reflection and assessment is inherently counterintuitive to our natural instinct - it's looking back when everything is screaming to look ahead. This is what makes reflection and assessment so crucial to success, as it often differentiates intentional individuals from simply reactive folks.

DOCUMENTING YOUR PROCESS

When we talk about moving in a healthier direction, as it relates to sustainable sexual integrity, you need to be able to identify new paths, insights, tools, and behaviors to see sustainable growth and change. Effectively, what is NEW about you, your mind, your responses, your cognitive patters, your inner voice, your toolkit, your awareness etc.

A couple age-old adages to consider...

> THE BEST INDICATOR OF FUTURE PERFORMANCE IS PAST BEHAVIOR.

> IF YOU ALWAYS DO WHAT YOU'VE ALWAYS DONE, YOU WILL ALWAYS GET WHAT YOU'VE ALWAYS GOT.

> INFORMATION – NOT PERSUASION – BUILDS TRUST.

If in relationship, I highly recommend documenting a process that can be transparent and reviewed in the context of a relationship, discussed with your partner. This new information, your newly documented process, can be a gift to a betrayed partner who can use your documented process to see how cravings and triggers will be overcome in the future (and so much more). Additionally, working together on what those processes will look like can be an incredibly connecting exercise.

Now, let's get into the two main components of your documented process: **preventative** and **acute**.

PREVENTATIVE

Preventative process: these are the things you do on a regular/daily basis to put yourself in a healthier place. These are your daily "multivitamins." Simply put, these measures are preventative, and **not** intended for a crisis situation.

This could look like journaling, going through your feelings wheel, a 1-10 check-in, practicing presence, a grounding exercise, taking a shower, doing the dishes, texting a friend hello, a gratitude list, stretching, etc.

One risk worth noting here - it's important to watch out for your preventative processes from becoming your identity. If you're on vacation, a work trip, or something else that renders you unable to engage in your preventative process, does your life fall apart? Do you fall apart? It's perfectly healthy to enjoy your process, however, one 'balancing metric' here is to ask yourself and I doing great or do I have a great process?

How will you know? If I remove your process form your routine are you a nightmare to be around? If so, your healthy is largely external. Essentially, don't rely solely on your preventative process. Allow your process to be a **support**, not a lonely life raft.

ACUTE

Acute process: these are the things you do in a moment of crisis, a sudden moment of heightened (not necessarily extreme) emotional difficulty, dysregulation, panic, discomfort or pain. To stick with our metaphor from above - this is calling the ambulance during a heart attack, not a multivitamin.

For many people, this is an opportunity to become aware of the fact there are two different types of process. I've worked with several clients who, during moments of extreme emotional pain, break out their preventative processes and find themselves further distressed when they provide no relief.

An acute crisis requires acute attention. These are your break-the-glass tools for relief.

It is critically important to understand - and document - what your process is for preventative measures and what is for acute needs. Using a perfect process at the wrong time will yield zero impact. Be sure to understand the difference.

SEEKING FAILURE

Fail fast. Fail often.

Contrary to most things in life, process is all about seeking failure. You want to fail as improvement is awaiting you on the other side. The goal is precisely to discover what doesn't work—the weak points and problem areas—because that's where the need is and therefore that is precisely where the growth happens.

This is **iterative process change.** You know from the very beginning that there is no such thing as a perfect process, and the best path forward is to document **any** process and work from there. The work will never be complete, you don't 'figure it out', you simply grow in your understanding, constantly developing and refining over time, but never closing yourself off to new possibilities. Ideally, a healthy individual does not engage in a process as a way to "reach the finish line," rather, they engage with their process because they're doing the work to show up for themselves and those in their life they care about, as well as their future self and the future loved ones they have yet to meet.

Your living and dynamic documented process is a receipt showing yourself and the world your intention.

Next, you'll document your process in the following pages. Multiple pages have been provided for you to return to, evaluate, and tweak as desired. There is no right or wrong process. Again, ask yourself: "What can I do to move in a healthier direction?"

DOCUMENT YOUR PROCESS EXERCISE:

<u>Instructions</u>: Both of these preventative and acute process items can be conducted both in retrospect as well as forward looking. In other words, this can be completed at the beginning of

your day or this can be concluded at the end of your day, both are fine. The below examples are simply one sit down, you could rinse and repeat as often as you'd like with each. Continue on a time cadence that continues to still provide value in your progress.

MY PREVENTATIVE PROCESS

- Today's Date:
- Daily Preventative Process Activities:
- Process Success Metric:
    - Who determined this metric?
- Outcome Success Metric:
    - Who determined this metric?
- When will I assess for a process tweak:

Notes & Takeaways:

MY ACUTE PROCESS

- Today's Date:
- Daily Acute Process Intervention Utilized:
- Process Success Metric:
    - Who determined this?
- Outcome Success Metric:
    - Who determined this?
- When will I assess for a process tweak:

Notes & Takeaways:

7

THE ADDICTION CYCLE
ANSWERING THE 'WHY'

The addiction cycle represented below is the single most comprehensive breakdown of 'how' a problematic sexual behavior pattern takes hold. The single most important exercise, tool and awareness lays at the feet of the addiction cycle. In your understanding and self-application of the addiction cycle to your specific behaviors and thought processes before, during and after acting you hold the keys to the proverbial kingdom. Here is where you will be able to answer the 'WHY' and 'HOW' that you and your partner or family are so desperately seeking answers to. I would go so far as to call a death grip level expertise on your own specific patterns along the addiction cycle a requirement to sustainable sexual integrity.

Understanding your pathological thoughts & actions - and their pattern - is paramount to self-expertise & thus sustainable sexual integrity.

In order to alleviate the effects of sex/porn addiction, you must first understand how this destructive and dysfunctional pattern occurs.

OVERVIEW

The cycle begins when a trigger or craving arises. Triggers exist outside of the addiction cycle and can act as an introduction or removal from the cycle. At their core, triggers are flags highlighting unattended needs and emotions that require resolution, relief or satisfaction generally.

Triggers often stem from emotions like fear, anxiety, worry, loneliness, abandonment, rejection, and neglect. It is critical to acknowledge the validity of these feelings, rather than treating them as something to be ignored or repressed. By comprehending the origins of your triggers, you give yourself the power to initiate a profound process of introspection and restoration.

Your first aim is to identify, understand, possibly confront and reconcile - or simply stay with - these emotions, preventing their likelihood of accumulating and reappearing to cause more harm in the future. Triggers are important to understand, as they can act as your entry into the addiction cycle. Pay attention to your triggers, study them, and evaluate their emotional origins.

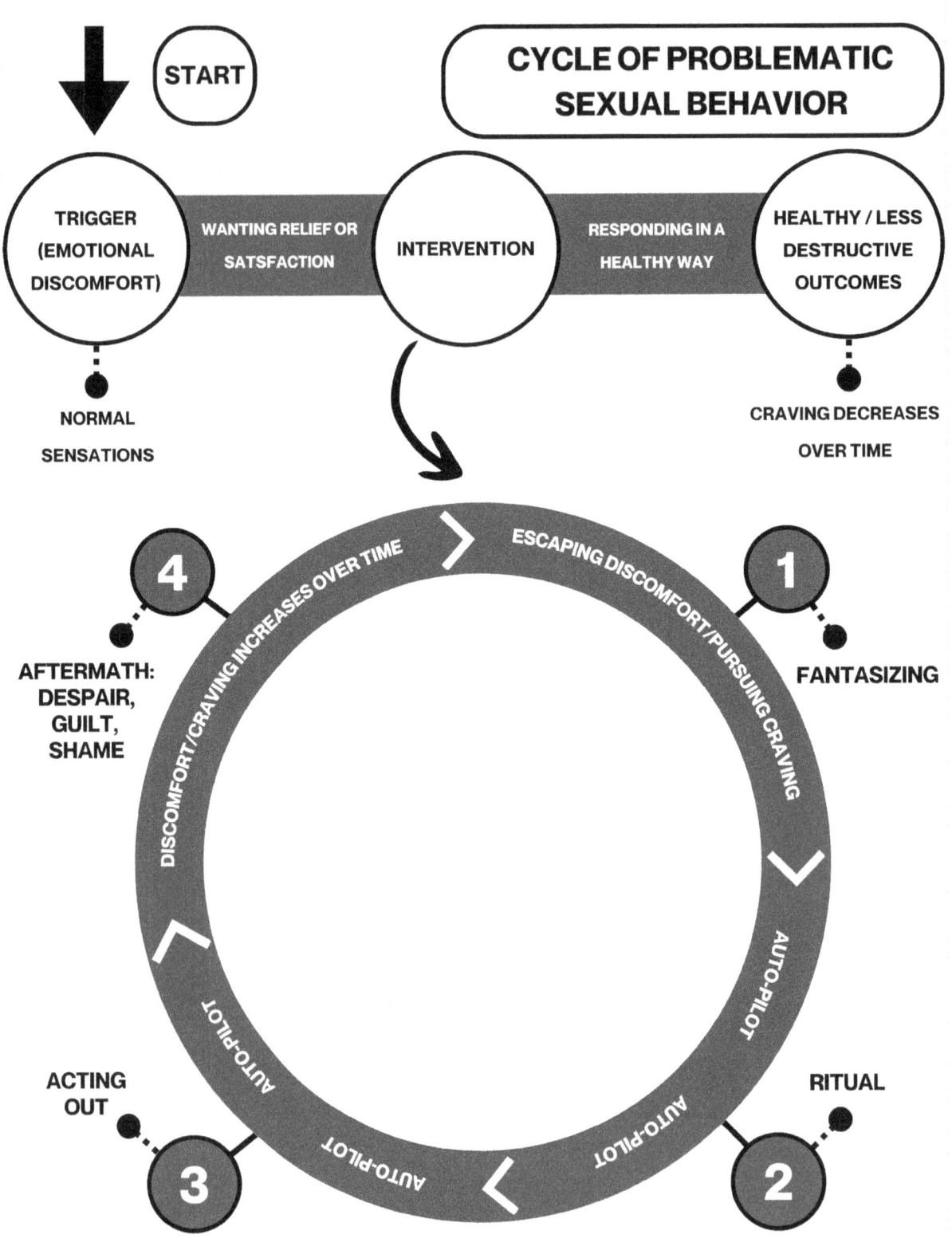

THE ADDICTION CYCLE

The Addiction Cycle, more specifically, is comprised of four phases:

Preoccupation

In this stage, an individual becomes preoccupied with an imagined reality. In contrast to fleeting thoughts, preoccupation is characterized by its excessive, all-consuming nature. This phase may be comparable in its intensity to the physical act of consuming pornography. Social isolation, diminished work performance, and increased distraction act as indicators and potential outcomes of preoccupation.

Ritualization

This phase is distinguished by the presence of repetitive patterns and behaviors exhibited by an individual prior to performing the act. This can manifest in explicit messaging or visitation of certain websites. The euphoria experienced during this stage can be exceptionally intense, emulating the high of consumption itself.

Utilization

This stage, building off the previous behaviors, signifies consumption.

Aftermath

Following the act of consumption, individuals commonly experience deep regret or despair as they confront the consequences of their behavior. Paradoxically, this emotional turmoil may propel the individual back to the first stage, preoccupation, thereby continuing the cycle of addiction.

In the addiction cycle, there is an initial decision-making juncture, otherwise referred to as a choice point. Here, you are confronted with the choice to either respond to your trigger in a healthy way or continue on through the cycle of addiction. The fundamental motivation of this decision frequently originates from a desire to mitigate the unease caused by a trigger/craving.

A constructive course of action is your firewall against a potential spiral. As part of your recovery process, you are going to begin building a defense plan to utilize at points of confrontation. The early part of this planning requires an investigation of the NEED that drives your problematic behavior. We need to understand how, in some way, your behavior has served as a solution for that need.

When a need arises, manifesting as a strong emotion, interrogate it. Use the feeling wheel.

What are you feeling? Lonely? Rejected? Once you gain an understanding of your emotions, you can see how, in the past, your behavior was actually "fixing" an emotion you felt. In this context, acting out actually makes sense. There's a rhyme and reason to your behavior.

This foundation of understanding paves the way for methods of intervention (your course of action to prevent problematic behavior) to be implemented. These healthy alternatives are targeted to meet the needs that have been historically solved through damaging, addictive behaviors. Going deeper, this next exercise will prompt you to explore your relationship with the following items:

Scenarios

Events and circumstances that can lead to potential relapse. Problematic scenarios are personal to each individual. What are the scenarios that increase your likelihood of acting out? Feeling lonely on a night in? Traveling for work? Identify them.

The Trigger

Most commonly the trigger is some form of emotional discomfort/tension/pain, likely experienced as cravings/thoughts/urges that have the potential to set off a cycle of problematic behavior.

Feel free to identify whatever other trigger you believe it to be for your lived experiences, however, I will encourage you strongly to lean into what difficult emotion was present for you.

Two errors most people make here:
1) They do not identify ALL of the various difficult emotions
2) They vilify the emotion

If you're feeling stressed, don't stop there, keep going! You're possibly also feeling overwhelmed, anxious, worried, exhausted, inadequate, resentful etc. No one ever only holds one feeling at a time - go deeper!!!

Don't vilify the feeling! The real question, why does that feeling bring up such pain at that precise moment?? Take for example the most common difficult emotion for men that comes up in my practice - inadequacy. Personally, I experience wild inadequacy the once a decade when I get dragged onto a golf course, yet I think it's hilarious. I laugh, others laugh, my inadequacy is borderline fun at those times. Now, put my in front of a group of students I'm lecturing or on stage at a conference and boy oh boy I do NOT enjoy inadequacy in those moments - I want to crawl under a rock when inadequacy hits me in those moments.

So, notice, the emotion itself isn't even the same within the same individual - in this case me. The very same emotion hits different within the same person based on the context among other things.

So, be sure not to take the easy way out by vilifying the feeling, instead go deeper, look (OBSERVE) through your past and consider how this particular emotion/s became so spicy in certain contexts, while maybe not so much in others.

The Need (wanting relief or satisfaction)

Incredibly important. If there is a trigger that is creating significant emotional pain, discomfort, tension or stress - be it acute or chronic (a SUPER important distinction), then what need is coming up for you - need for what? This is often incredibly confusing at the beginning and I believe that's because we overcomplicate it.

"Why did I do this?!" Is such a huge question that it makes sense that everyone if seeking a big answer. However, reframe your thinking on the topic of 'need.' Oxygen is a need. Water. A roof. Warmth. Clothing. Connection. These are all needs and are all incredibly simple. I would strongly advise against overcomplicating your understanding of needs arising within simply because others are not satisfied with your present understanding of your need. I promise you will never figure it out fully, so everyone can live the grey space of never fully and truly knowing, yet we are going to work within the best information that we have to date.

To get back to the need, consider the most common scenario I come across which is quite simply a NEED FOR RELIEF from emotional pain, tension or discomfort.

The need is simple... RELIEF!

Relief from what is the million dollar question, however I'd propose that even that lies at the simple idea of inner tension, pain or discomfort. But, let's forge ahead in breaking this down further.

The reason that this is so crucial, is if I am correct in proposing that there is a legitimate need arising within you, well then guess what, that need has to be met - it has to be resolved - and if you want create a path to meeting that need then your brain and body will step in to resolve, relieve that discomfort thus eliminating the perceived threat so that you may continue to function in a healthy way.

Example, if you're feeling inadequate at work - you're always behind, you're feeling inadequate as a partner - you don't make enough, aren't present enough, forget to make the reservation, etc, you've put on weight or your hair thinned out and aren't feeling as attractive as you used to, more inadequacy. At this point you're walking around the planet with a CHRONIC stressor, the emotional pain of chronic inadequacy is resting on your head and shoulders constantly. Now, while you may minimize this (eg. Doesn't this happen to everyone), your brain and body find these tensions difficult for functioning - maintaining sleep, relationships, ability to succeed at tasks/job etc.) this tension needs to be relieved so that functioning may resume.
This is sometimes referred to as the 'FIX', however I prefer to focus on the humanness and the needs that arise within the individual.

Intervention
Once we've advanced in our ability to understand the need, how do we shift our response to a less destructive response that arrives closer at meeting the need? This is our intervention.

Think of it this way, without an intervening force the same patterns will always play out. The hope is that by attempting a new intervention once may meet the need arising within via less dysfunctional method.

What are your strategies for preventing a spiral into the addiction cycle?

Most often, individuals are more focused on distracting themselves, puttering, being productive, staying busy - do anything but be still with the craving/thought/urge. The trouble is, of course, not only is this fear-based methodology but it's not sustainable. One cannot forever be busy. One cannot distract forever. It is not operating from an empowered position. The thought is dictating how the individuals day must go, not the individual dictating terms to their thoughts.

Interventions not only meet the underlying need in less destructive ways that acting out (notice I'm not starting out even saying healthy, simply less destructive), but effective interventions return the person back to a place of empowerment and strength, not fear or imprisonment.

To change behavior successfully, effective intervention is required. If an intervention does not occur, the best indicator of future performance is past behavior.

The brain, the body, and the individual can all make future predictions based on what has happened in the past. More specifically, you remember what has successfully relieved, resolved, or satisfied your triggers in the past, and you know these methods will work again. For many, this is when behavior begins to feel compulsive, or uncontrollable. It may feel as if intervention is impossible, or you "don't have a choice." The instinct to act-out is almost reflective, occurring without thought.

For some, the "work" here is very simply understanding that an opportunity to intervene is available and attainable. For others, who feel their behavior is uncontrollable and impulsive, the work begins by understanding the various links in the chain leading up to triggers and problematic behavior.

SELF-APPLICATION: ADDICTION CYCLE

Now, take what you've learned and apply your own lived experience and patterns to the cycle in the exercise below. Think back on your life and exhaustively outline as many problematic scenarios as you can think of, then consider WITHIN that specific scenario (we'll call it Scenario 1), what do you believe the trigger - or multiple triggers within a single scenario - to be, then what do you believe the need to be and lastly, what intervention could you have deployed that MIGHT have possibly worked to meet the need as opposed to acting out. Be exhaustive in this effort, I can assure you that the juice is most definitely worth the squeeze here.

∼

SCENARIO 1

<u>What is the scenario?</u> (*Eg. Work travel, up alone at night, bored, etc.*)

<u>What are the trigger/s in this specific scenario?</u> (*Eg. Emotional pain form loneliness*)

<u>What is the *need* in this specific scenario?</u> (relief, satisfaction, etc.)

_____

_____

What interventions help/could help in this specific scenario?

_____

_____

_____

_____

SCENARIO 2

What is the scenario?

_____

_____

_____

What are the triggers associated with this scenario?

_____

_____

_____

What is the *need* in this scenario? (relief, satisfaction, etc.)

_____

_____

_____

_____

What interventions can you leverage when this scenario arises?

_____

_____

_____

SCENARIO 3

What is the scenario?

_____

_____

_____

What are the triggers associated with this scenario?

_____

_____

_____

What is the *need* in this scenario? (relief, satisfaction, etc.)

SELF-APPLICATION: ADDICTION CYCLE

What interventions can you leverage when this scenario arises?

SCENARIO 4

What is the scenario?

What are the triggers associated with this scenario?

What is the *need* in this scenario? (relief, satisfaction, etc.)

_____

_____

_____

_____

What interventions can you leverage when this scenario arises?

_____

_____

_____

_____

SCENARIO 5

What is the scenario?

_____

_____

_____

What are the triggers associated with this scenario?

_____

_____

SELF-APPLICATION: ADDICTION CYCLE

What is the *need* in this scenario? (relief, satisfaction, etc.)

What interventions can you leverage when this scenario arises?

DEFENSE MECHANISMS
ANSWERING "HOW COULD YOU DO THAT?!"

Individuals engaging in dysfunctional and destructive sexual behavior patterns often leverage defense mechanisms - rationalizations - to cope with and justify their harmful behaviors. Defense mechanisms allow you to do two things: rationalize harmful or morally incongruent behavior and perpetuate the behavior. Though instinctual, these mechanisms can reinforce negative beliefs about yourself and others and keep the patterns embedded.

The most common defense mechanisms leveraged in sexual acting out are minimization, entitlement, compartmentalization then denial (when all else fails).

In overcoming problematic sexual behavior, it's crucial to recognize and acknowledge your own utilization of defense mechanisms. In this chapter, we'll explore each of these "rationalization strategies" individually, as well as the role they play in the grand scheme of your unique pathology.

To develop a full understanding of these mechanisms, it is important to cultivate an atmosphere that allows for introspection and impartial observation. Encourage yourself to observe thoughts and emotions without immediate response or repression. The aim is to properly identify defense mechanisms in order to adequately deconstruct them in your own life.

"HOW COULD YOU DO THIS?! I DON'T KNOW WHO YOU ARE!"

Your partner may have asked you:

"You must not love me - how could you do this and still love me? I don't even know who you are."

This is a fantastic question, a common questions. It's a completely normal, healthy, question that must be answered for trust to be built. The individual dealing with problematic sexual behavior has to be able to answer this question for themselves to fully achieve sustainable sexual integrity.

This question, reframed, might sound more like: *"How could I have done so many hurtful things to the people I love and care about?"* This question needs to be answered - as a requirement - in order to advance in one's recovery and relationships.

Other questions that follow a similar line of thought might be:

"Have you ever been the person I thought you were?"
"How could you do this?"
"Who are you?"

This is often where shame, guilt, despair, and internalization set in. Without a good answer to these questions, the individual blames themselves for their shortcomings. In reality, we have two options: either the individual did these things for no good reason, or they did these things for a very good reason.

Most often, problematic behavior serves as an incredibly efficient solution for some discomfort. However, once the behavior is done, the individual works hard to rationalize away the potential devastation of said behavior. Rationalization by way of defense mechanisms is what makes an individual able to act out in intensely devastating ways and then lay next to their partner at night.

The tricky part about defense mechanisms is that once the brain discovers an effective method of rationalization, the method continues to be utilized and new defense mechanisms are not sought out. Before we dive into the complexities of each, let's examine the five primary defense mechanisms found in sex and porn addiction.

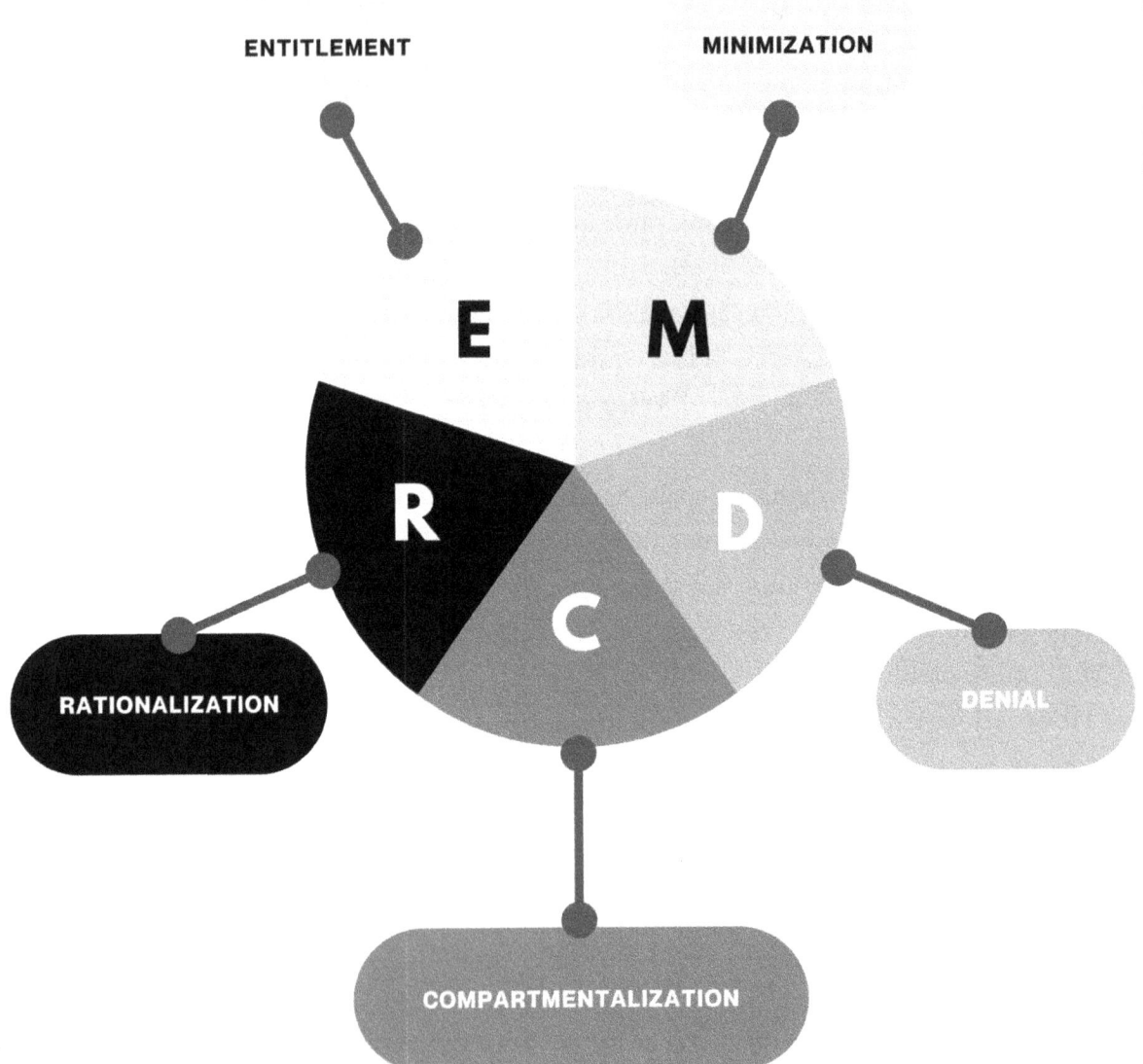

MINIMIZATION

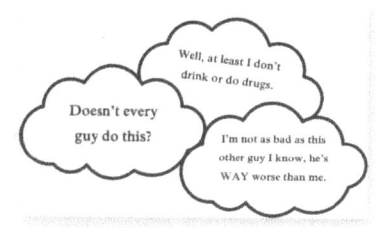

Minimizing ones behavior, or its effects. This may involve dismissing concerns about your behavior or telling yourself "things aren't as bad as they seem." When we look at problematic sexual behavior, we typically see a progression of defense mechanisms. This usually starts with minimization. It's important to note that there's still an acknowledgment and ownership of the behavior present within minimization. There is simply a "good reason" that helps the individual rationalize the behavior. So, there is an element of awareness of a "problem" with this defense mechanism. Minimization is by far the most common mechanism leveraged in sex and porn addiction.

ENTITLEMENT

The idea that one has the "right" to engage in sexual behavior no matter the consequences or effects on others. This can lead to a lack of empathy. After minimization, we often see entitlement. With entitlement, there is still a sense of awareness and ownership of the behavior present. The rationalization happens by, once again, asserting a "good reason" to engage in potentially destructive behavior.

COMPARTMENTALIZATION

Hiding sexual behavior or maintaining a "public persona." This can help in avoiding shame or guilt, but prevents one from seeing how their actions affect others. With compartmentalization, the individual begins to move in a direction where there is less ownership over the behavior, though there is certainly an acknowledgment of its existence. Compartmentalization can actually be healthy in various aspects of life—think of an emergency room doctor who deals regularly with death going home to eat dinner with their family. However, when an individual compartmentalizes to avoid examining their unhealthy behavioral patterns or unmet needs (tension, pain, discomfort), it becomes dangerous and problematic.

RATIONALIZATION

Excuse-making, can look like telling yourself that certain sexual behaviors are necessary for relief or "not hurting anyone." Rationalization is used to provide good reasons for problematic behavior. It defends against feelings of guilt and allows one to maintain a level of self-respect. Often, one curates their own set of "facts" that allows them to continue perpetuating the behavior.

DENIAL

Avoidance of reality. This can look like minimizing behavior or avoiding conversations or situations that may force one to confront their addiction. When an individual is in a state of denial, they are, in a sense, protected from the problem they're avoiding and its consequences. This individual may become irritable or dismissive when the subject of a problem is even broached. Denial can manifest both internally and externally.

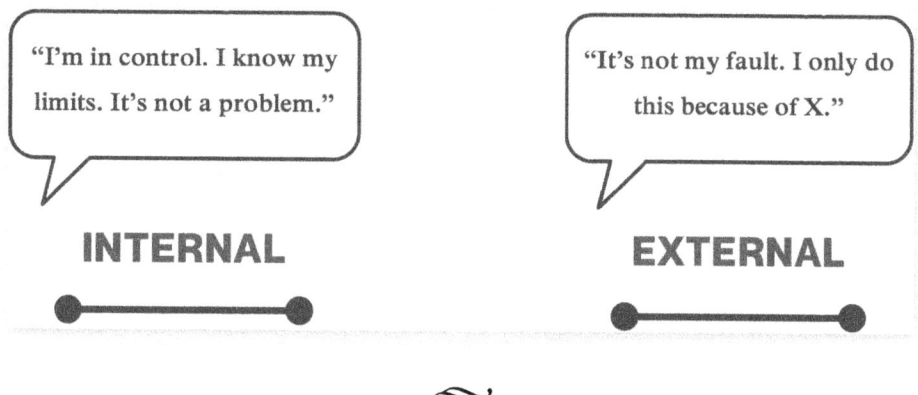

WHY DO WE RATIONALIZE?

So, why does the brain work so hard to rationalize behavior instead of moving in a healthier direction? This is a great question that must be accounted for. These rationalizations bring with them immeasurable pain once problematic behavior surfaces. To take a step back, consider another question: What is the brain's ultimate function? The answer is efficient survival.

Our brain, constantly scanning our environment for threats, leads us to the reasonable assumption that full transparency in any relationship might bring with it considerable tension or strife. In many relationships, it is not ridiculous to say that transparency (about cravings, desires, etc.) might bring tension that drastically affects one's relationship and living situation. At which point, the individual is left without their support structure, a place to lay their head, or any sense of safety and stability.

For this reason, it makes perfect sense why the brain would scan all of these threats and decide against transparency, instead, moving toward a path of survivability through concealment. Through secrecy and rationalization, the brain eliminates all immediate threats, focused on the most efficient path of survival, not concerned with potentially greater effects that may arise further down the line.

INTRINSIC MOTIVATION

WHO GETS TO DECIDE HOW YOUR DAY GOES? YOUR BOSS? YOUR PARTNER?
Ultimately, sustainable sexual integrity is dependent upon your empowerment. If you live your life at the whim of external factors (other people, seasons of the year, traffic jams), and allow these things to determine the quality of your day, sustainable sexual integrity will never be attainable. In this chapter, we'll examine the concept of intrinsic vs. extrinsic motivation.

To start, lets evaluate your current balance of extrinsic variables (items entirely out of your control) and intrinsic variables (items in your control). Is your life comprised of primarily extrinsic items? If so, it's no surprise for you to feel overwhelmed, vulnerable, and out of control—because you are.

If a majority of your variables are extrinsic, then a majority of your life is going to be driven by factors outside of your domain. Knowing and understanding your balance is an incredible opportunity to move in a healthier direction and start reorienting your sources of validation inward.

EXTRINSIC (BEYOND MY CONTROL)

The good news: acknowledging the extrinsic factors in your life and labeling them as such releases you from any delusion of control over these uncontrollable items. It may seem counterintuitive, but accepting the simple fact that some things are out of your control can be incredibly empowering. Up until today, you may have gone through life confused and frustrated, asking questions like: Why isn't my life getting better? Why aren't things improving? And offering yourself as the answer.

In this next exercise, you'll work to identify the extrinsic factors in your life and begin to lift the burden of self-blame. Beyond acknowledgment, it's important to examine each factor and determine your power to either reduce or eliminate them. Maybe at work, you're required to sit in on a committee that brings you considerable discomfort and stress each week. This would be an extrinsic factor of pain in your life. Your job, now, is to determine your ability to reduce the footprint of this factor.

Ultimately, your place on the committee is explicitly out of your control. However, you can evaluate ways in which to reduce the footprint of its impact on your life. Can you talk to your boss about reducing your role on the committee? Can you reduce the footprint, even a little bit? Or, maybe you determine that this committee is the single greatest driver of difficult emotion in your life. Then, it might be appropriate to remove the committee from your life entirely.

INTRINSIC (IN MY CONTROL)

Like extrinsic items, intrinsic variables are drivers of your difficult emotions. However, these are items that you have a semblance of control over. Something to note here is the common confusion around variables that involve another individual. Some people are inclined to evaluate their variables self-critically, assuming fault or responsibility in triggering situations involving other people. For example, you might have a difficult boss at work who writes you up, reprimands and critiques you consistently. Understandably, you might identify this variable as intrinsic, thinking, "I could have done better."

When another human being is involved, its important to allow them their autonomy. Many bosses, in the same situation, might not have written you up. But for whatever reason, this boss, at this time, chose to do so. The actions of others exist outside of your control, and it's important that you assign yourself blame only when it is appropriate and productive to do so. It's possible for both "I can try harder at work" and "The actions of my boss are beyond my control" to exist at the same time.

In the following exercise, you're going to begin by identifying your most difficult emotions and the factors that drive these emotions, both intrinsic and extrinsic. Don't worry too much about categorizing these drivers as you start—instead, tap into the feelings that bring you intense discomfort and work to understand what is causing this discomfort.

ARE YOU IN CONTROL?

Step One
On the next page, write down five primary emotions that bring you difficulty or discomfort. Refer to The Feeling Wheel on page 26. On an average day, which emotions most frequently cause frustration, cravings, and irritability for you?

Step Two
Below each emotion, write down what you believe to be the primary drivers of that emotion. If inadequacy is one of your problematic emotions, then ask yourself, what makes you feel inadequate? If some days you feel inadequate and some days you don't, what's the difference between those days? That's your driver. Some drivers of inadequacy might be: gaining weight, being late to work, not meeting your sobriety goals, etc. List as many drivers as you like: it never hurts to understand what's causing a difficult emotion.

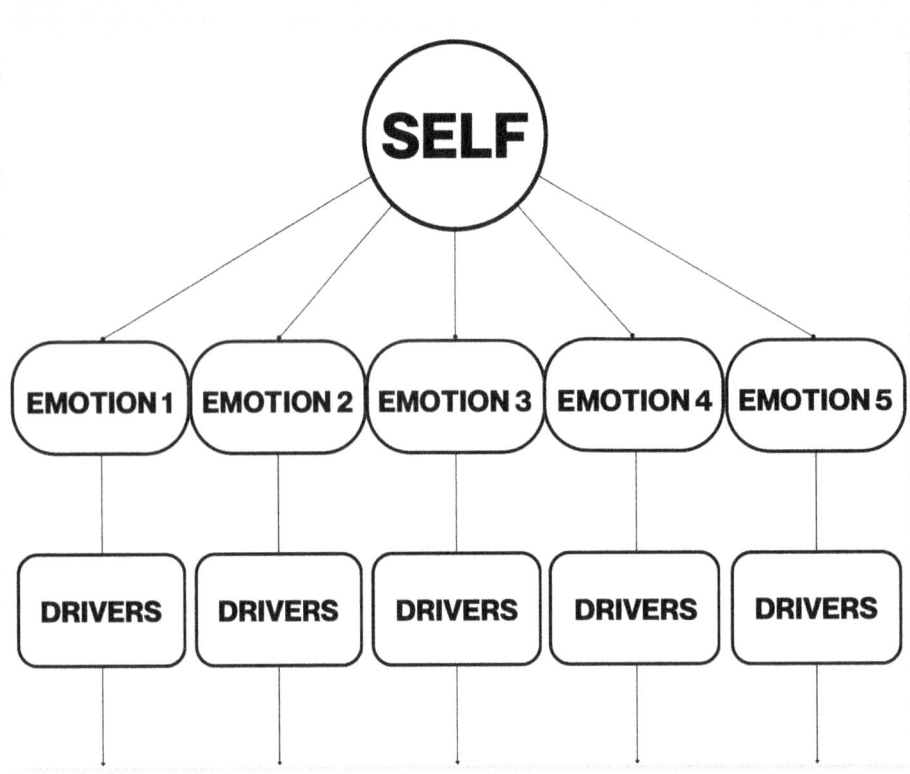

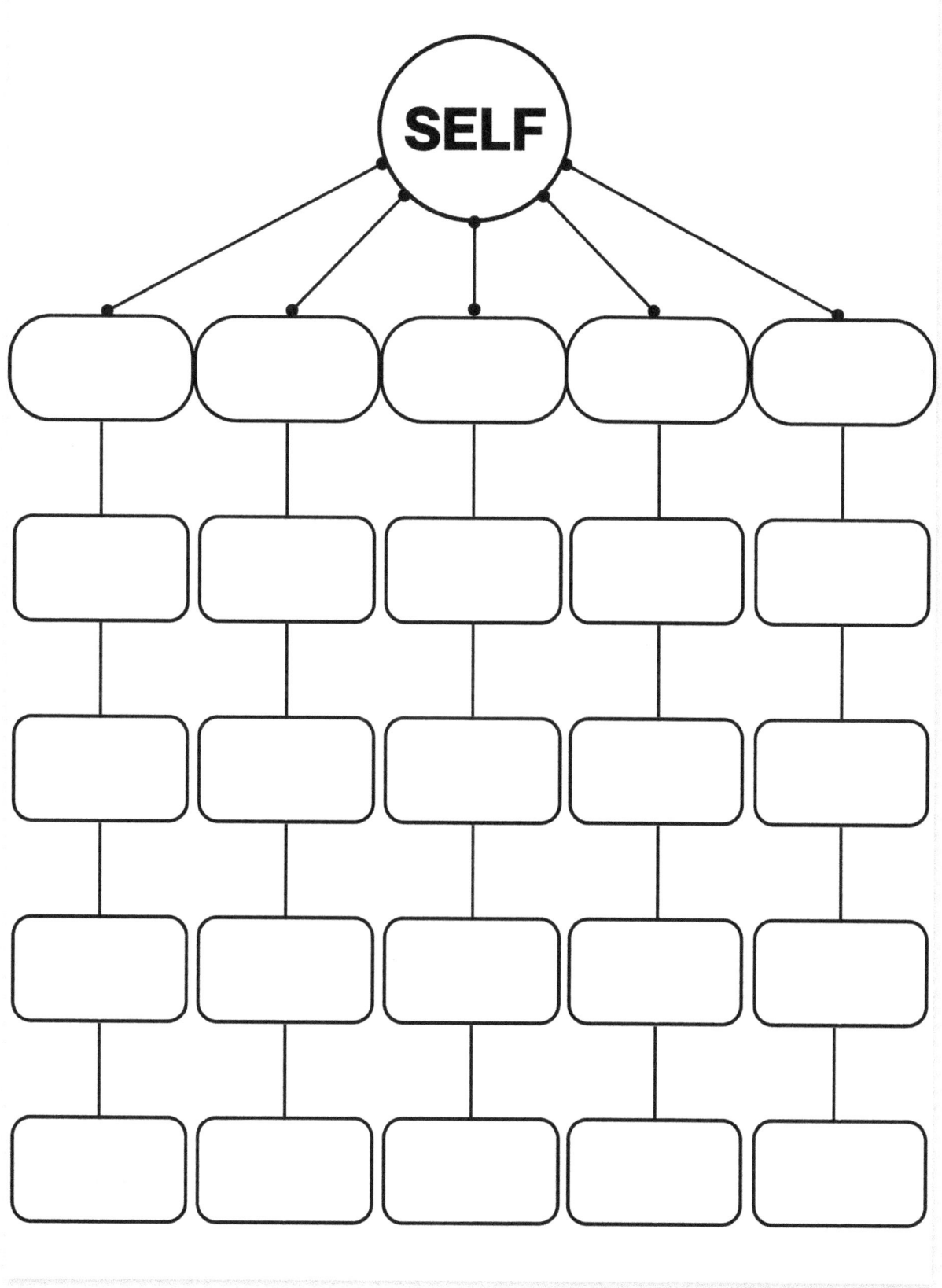

ARE YOU IN CONTROL?

Step Three
Now, with your primary emotions and drivers listed, break out a Sharpie and circle drivers that are extrinsic. Ask yourself: is this driver within or beyond my control?

Step Four
Add up the total amount of drivers listed. Then, calculate the percentage of intrinsic and extrinsic variables listed (e.g., 8 extrinsic drivers/20 total drivers = 40% extrinsic, 60% intrinsic). What's your ratio of extrinsic items to intrinsic items? Are you largely influenced by items within your control? Or are your emotions being driven by external factors? If your extrinsic items make up more than 50%, it might help to explain why you feel out of control.

Step Five
Consider your intrinsic drivers (items within your control). What can you do to minimize their effect on your emotional world? Then, take a look at the extrinsic variables you've listed. Is there any room for you to reduce or eliminate their effects?

How can I work on my **intrinsic** drivers?

_____

_____

_____

_____

_____

_____

_____

ARE YOU IN CONTROL?

How can I work on my **extrinsic** drivers?

WHEN WE WORK ON ALTERING BEHAVIOR, IT'S BEST TO TAKE IT ONE STEP AT A TIME. Start simple: focus on one change at a time. In recovery work, a tackle-everything-at-once approach is known as "The Grand Gesture." With this attempt, one might: wake up an hour early, exercise an hour more, opt for a cold shower, drink all black coffee, and make every meal at home, all at once.

It's exciting to make changes that are within your control. But typically, sudden and overwhelming change is going to fall apart once some time passes and the excitement is gone. To maintain the motivation, try implementing these alterations one at a time, giving each change the attention it deserves. This gives you time and wisdom to observe the impact of each change, and allows you to tweak your process as you go. A handy rule is to allot one week for each new change in your process.

9

SHAME & INTERNALIZATION

Most men, when they start attempting to overcome problematic sexual behavior, view themselves as the "problem." They believe there's something inherently wrong, flawed, or broken within them—and this is what is driving their problematic behavior, despite all efforts and intentions to stop. When you continue to engage in a pattern of behavior that doesn't align with your values or concept of self without understanding **why**, the easiest answer is to blame yourself.

Clinically, this is known as internalization. When you fail to find an answer for some pattern of behavior, you assign yourself as the answer, assuming the problem as originating within yourself. At this point, when an individual places the blame on themselves and views this "problem" as a weakness or character flaw, incredible shame begins to show up on the heels of this internalization.

As one continues to blame themselves for this continuing pattern of behavior, they naturally begin to deal with all kinds of self-critical thinking, shame, and doubt. And, as all of these painful emotions are coming up, the most simple path to relief is found in familiar behaviors that have proven to relieve emotional pain in the past. This is what keeps an individual returning to problematic behavior, and what keeps them trapped in such a harmful cycle.

Shame and internalization are sustainability killers. So, let's tackle them one at a time. This chapter will explore the complexities of both, and what to do about them. But, essentially, in order to resolve internalization we simply need **a good answer**. If I have a good answer for my behavior, it's a lot easier to take the blame off myself. As for shame, we'll work to build shame resilience first and foremost.

INTERNALIZATION

Consider this analogy. Imagine you're driving on the highway and somebody zooms in at full speed and cuts you off. You're taken aback, filled with all kinds of anxiety, anger, frustration, and vulnerability at the thought of what might've happened due to someone's reckless driving. All of these emotions are understandable.

Now, imagine the driver of that car. Imagine you discover that the person who cut you off was a man driving his wife to the hospital as she was going into labor, desperately trying to reach medical assistance for the delivery of a healthy and happy baby. I'm willing to bet that this piece of information offers a significant opportunity to reshape those emotions of frustration and anger that came from being cut off in traffic.

Understanding **why** a behavior took place can drastically alter your experience and perspective of an event. This is very much the case with acting out. Without a good answer to explain why you're acting out, it's logical to assume that there's something inside of you causing the problem.

This is especially dangerous early in one's recovery, as research has shown that cold-turkey abstinence does not lead to success without an understanding of the behavior's original cause. Within this formula, we'll call this lack of understanding a **lack of autonomy**: an insufficient knowledge of where problematic behavior originates and why it has been sustained despite one's stated values, desires, and sense of self. So:

Abstinence - Autonomy = Increased Depression + Increased Thoughts of Self-Harm

There's no harm, necessarily, in quitting "cold turkey," so long as one moves quickly away from internalization. The first step of this might look like simply appreciating the possibility of other contributing factors at play beyond personal failure. The endgame, down the road, is to blow up internalization for good by identifying the true drivers of patterned behavior and the **need** behind those drivers. Ultimately, there is a need within the individual, not a failure, that must be met. To meet this need, we simply need to understand what it is, why it is, and begin to craft interventions to meet the need in less destructive ways.

It's commonly thought that this approach serves as an abdication of one's ownership or accountability for past behaviors and consequences. This idea suggests that an individual is seeking an escape, or attempting to "blame" everything on their childhood, trauma, or other outside sources. It's important to understand that this is **not** the case.

To find a sustainable path forward, one must move in the direction of becoming an expert on themselves. The best way to gain self-expertise is to understand all the different facets and variables that make you **you**. You must explore these variables and how they interact with each other thoroughly: when did they show up? How have they shifted over time? Have they been more or less destructive at different points in time, or generally consistent? The goal is to understand these variables from every possible angle to the best of your ability at this point in time.

This is how you stop internalization. Increase your knowledge and awareness—so you can build a roadmap forward, meeting the underlying need in less harmful ways.

SHAME

Now, let's shift our focus to shame, and more importantly: shame resilience, vulnerability, and its tie to sustainable sobriety. Here, I'd like to point to the foremost expert researcher on shame, shame resilience, and vulnerability, Brené Brown. Let's use her work to help carve a path to sustainable sexual sobriety.

Brené Brown's Shame Resilience Theory (SRT) provides a framework for moving away from shame-based coping mechanisms (such as addiction, compulsive behaviors, and self-destructive habits) and into vulnerability, connection, and healing. Here, we'll outline her principles of shame resilience and explore how these can be applied to your daily life.

THE FOUR CORE ELEMENTS OF SHAME RESILIENCE IN RECOVERY

1. **Recognizing Shame and Understanding Its Triggers**

Sustainable sobriety requires awareness of the emotional states and experiences that lead to shame-driven behaviors. Common shame "triggers" in addiction and compulsive behavior include:

- Failing to meet self-imposed expectations of "perfection" in recovery.
- Feeling unworthy of love, connection, or healing.
- Relapsing or struggling with cravings and self-judgment.

Recovery Application:

- Begin tracking when shame surfaces—note what events, thoughts, or feelings precede urges to engage in self-destructive behaviors.

- Develop an early warning system for emotional relapse (e.g., self-isolation, negative self-talk, feeling like a burden).

2. **Practicing Critical Awareness**

Shame loses power when we recognize that it is often tied to external pressures, false beliefs, and unrealistic expectations. Many people in recovery internalize societal messages that addiction is a moral failure rather than a complex, treatable issue.

Recovery Application:

- Challenge internalized stigma—remind yourself that addiction is not about weakness but about coping with pain in ineffective ways.
- Normalize setbacks as part of the healing journey rather than a reason to spiral into self-blame. Identify and reframe unhealthy beliefs such as:
- "I will never be good enough." → "Recovery is about progress, not perfection."
- "I'm broken." → "Healing is possible, and I am worthy of it."

3. **Reaching Out and Speaking Shame**

Shame thrives in secrecy, while connection and honesty dissolve it. Many people relapse because they try to manage their struggles alone instead of reaching out.

Recovery Application:

- Engage in open, honest communication with a therapist, sponsor, support group, or trusted friend.
- Practice saying, "I'm struggling," instead of isolating when shame arises.
- Attend group meetings (e.g., 12-step, SMART Recovery, therapy groups) to break the cycle of shame through shared experiences.
- Use a journal or voice memos if verbalizing shame feels too difficult at first.

4. **Practicing Empathy and Self-Compassion**

Sustainable sobriety is not just about abstaining from problematic behaviors but about learning to treat oneself with kindness. Many people "self-medicate" to escape deep-seated self-criticism or lack of self-worth.

Recovery Application:

- Speak to yourself with the same compassion you would offer a friend in recovery.
- Replace self-punishment with self-care practices that reinforce worthiness (e.g., meditation, exercise, rest, creative outlets).
- Use affirmations rooted in self-compassion:
- "I am worthy of healing."
- "I can make mistakes and still be lovable."
- "Recovery is not about never falling but about learning to get back up."

ADDITIONAL SHAME RESILIENCE STRATEGIES FOR SUSTAINABLE SOBRIETY

1. **Developing a Shame Resilience Practice**

- Awareness first! Utilize the daily check-ins to notice shame patterns and choose vulnerability over avoidance.
- Practice self-awareness exercises like mindfulness, breathwork, or grounding techniques (options found in chapter 2).

2. **Understanding the Difference Between <u>Guilt</u> and <u>Shame</u>**

- Guilt says, "I made a mistake." (Can lead to growth and change).
- Shame says, "I *am* a mistake." (Leads to isolation and self-sabotage).
- Recovery requires reframing mistakes as learning opportunities rather than evidence of unworthiness.

3. **Building Shame Awareness in Relationships**

- Many in recovery fear judgment from loved ones, which can trigger relapse.
- Engage in open conversations about shame and vulnerability with trusted people.
- Learn to set boundaries with people who reinforce shame-based thinking.

4. **Avoiding Shame Triggers from Perfectionism**

- Recovery is not about doing it "perfectly"—there is no perfect way to heal.

- Progress over perfection: every small step forward counts.

5. **Using Courage to Break the Silence**

- Share struggles before they escalate into a relapse.
- Challenge the belief that needing support is a weakness.
- Choose authenticity over hiding pain.

6. **Owning Your Story**

- Healing comes from integrating past experiences without letting them define your future.
- Practice radical self-acceptance: "I am not my worst mistakes; I am who I choose to become."

7. **Surrounding Yourself with Empathetic People**

- Stay connected with people who encourage healing rather than reinforce self-destructive patterns.
- Find a sponsor, therapist, or mentor who models shame resilience.

8. **Practicing Self-Compassion**

- Self-compassion is the antidote to self-loathing and the key to long-term recovery.
- Replace shame-based narratives with empowering ones:
- Instead of "I'm too weak to recover," say "Healing is a process, and I am strong enough to keep going."

9. **Setting Boundaries Against Shame-Based Expectations**

- Recognize when cultural, family, or personal expectations create shame.
- Set limits with toxic environments that reinforce self-hatred or addiction triggers.

10. **Challenging Unrealistic Cultural Expectations**

- Many people struggle with shame from societal expectations (e.g., men should never show weakness, high-achievers should never struggle).

- Recovery involves rejecting these rigid norms and embracing authenticity.

11. **Turning Vulnerability into Strength**

    - Vulnerability is not weakness—it is the path to real connection and healing.
    - Those who recover successfully are those who allow themselves to be seen and supported.

12. **Embracing Authenticity**

    - Healing requires stepping into one's true self, free from shame-based masks.
    - The more you align with your values and truth, the less likely you are to return to old patterns of escape.

Brené Brown's work teaches that shame is a major driver of destructive behavior patterns, including problematic sexual behavior and compulsive cycles. Sustainable sexual sobriety is not just about avoiding harmful behaviors—it is about transforming one's relationship with self-worth, vulnerability, and connection. By applying Brown's shame resilience strategies, individuals in recovery can move away from shame-driven triggers and into a more authentic, fulfilling, and connected life.

10

SAFE VULNERABILITY

"IS IT SAFE TO BE ME?"

Let's now turn our attention to how we connect to other human beings via interpersonal relationships and human connections. The big idea we're aiming to understand is how intimacy, one's childhood, and parenting style experienced interact with and contribute to problematic sexual behavior. Additionally, we'll be looking at experiences of neglect, abuse, and trauma as we seek to connect the dots within the variables at play. These are *massive* subjects that cannot be fully understood within a few chapters, so we're going to focus on the central question involved.

I would propose that the closer one gets to answering this question, the closer they are to to understanding their behavioral patterns and underlying needs, which is, of course, our blueprint to sustainable sexual integrity. Even understanding the layers of this question provides clarity in recovery, let alone finding a response to it. In comprehending the relationship between one's destructive behavioral patterns and their own concept of self, this question is singularly fundamental:

- **When did I first feel unsafe simply being myself?**
- **When did I first feel unaccepted for who I was?**
- **When did I first realize that being myself was not okay, that I needed to add or subtract something to be okay/safe/accepted in this moment?**

For those keeping score at home, your math is correct. That was three questions, not one, but I'd propose they're the same question in different forms. Now pause, and try to answer it:

Was it when you were scolded as a child for having your elbows on the dinner table? Or blowing bubbles in your milk? At five years old, you thought it would be a *blast* to blow bubbles in your milk, watching them rise to the rim of the glass—how cool!

But Mom or Dad had other feelings, making it obvious that what felt perfectly normal to you was *not* okay in this setting. In that moment, you learned acutely that your natural, organic feeling was not okay. You probably weren't even sure why, but you learned to **subtract** this behavior in this moment. It, simply, was not okay to be you.

Now, to be clear, I'm not saying this is any form of neglect from the parent. However, in moments like these, while one's young mind is still forming, the child receives the message loud and clear. Of course, we must consider how the message is communicated, but ultimately, the child learns that it's not okay to move about the world freely and that they may need to be something other than their natural selves.

I remember one day, taking my 6-year-old son to school when he was having a particularly hard time transitioning out of weekend-mode and into school-mode (which is understandable). We had had an exceptional weekend filled with wrestling, a trip to GameStop, a SpongeBob Lego set, a ride through the car wash, and our Sunday morning tradition of blueberry and chocolate chip Belgian waffles. After a weekend like that, who would want to be stuck inside a boring classroom (or office, for most of us) all day?

The kid was raising a very good point as to why Monday seemed like a terrible idea. My job, as a parent, was to do the best I could to validate these feelings and help him understand that it's perfectly normal for this transition to be difficult, and (at the same time) we still need to move forward in a direction that is healthiest for us. On that day, for him and me, what was healthy for us was school and work, respectively.

This doesn't change the fact that everything going on inside of him was perfectly normal, appropriate, and healthy. But, it wasn't going to change the outcome—he needed to go to school. But on that day, my job was to make him feel safe enough to *feel* those difficult feelings and be with him through that emotional discomfort.

Once we get to school, he starts getting really emotional. He begins to cry, overwhelmed by his emotions and not quite sure what to do with them. As we get to the door of his classroom, his teacher says to him, "Come on buddy, big boys don't cry."

This was devastating to me, as it completely unwound all the work I had just done to validate his feelings, make him feel safe, and help him understand that we're *allowed* to feel big, difficult emotions. That we can find ways to navigate these emotions by identifying them and moving forward in the healthiest direction for us. The teacher was sending the message that is was not safe to be him: his feelings and emotions were not appropriate (for his gender, in this case), and there was something wrong with him feeling those feelings.

So now, in this moment, this child is rattled with big, difficult emotions that he's struggling to identify because he's six years old, and he's having trouble understanding what to *do* with these big feelings. On top of that, he's now being told that it is not safe for him to simply be himself or feel those feelings in this moment.

I certainly don't mean to pick on this teacher—God love 'em for spending time with my unruly wild child each day. I'm certain that *that* message had been handed down to them like some kind of terrible inheritance. However, I use this illustration to point out how early we might receive these messages that it is not safe to be ourselves. I also share this example because I believe it's important to highlight the impossibility of my son even remembering this small interaction with his teacher. However, this small interaction still has the ability to significantly impact how he feels about himself and his emotions, which is the kind of weight that can be carried throughout life if not addressed.

Maybe it came later for you, in middle or high school, on a sports team or in drama club, and you learned that something about you was not okay and needed to be different. Maybe it was when you started dating, and you found yourself shapeshifting to be what you thought your partner wanted you to be.

By no means am I promoting unbridled, lawless parenting or a society without boundaries as a means to avoid making anyone feel unsafe. I am simply proposing that crucial impact of validation and safety in one's early life. And, when all else fails, the superpower of repair—the ability to follow up when the best *you* fails to show up.

PARENTING STYLE

Next, let's take a look at the type of household one grows up in, as well as the relationship between different parenting styles and one's experience with problematic sexual behavior.

The Augustine Fellowship has published research indicating that nearly 90% of individuals who meet criteria for compulsive sexual behavior disorder grow up in either rigid or disengaged households (Derbyshire & Grant, 2015). A rigid home would look something like, "my house, my rules," while a disengaged household would be a home where you may *know* you're loved, but aren't shown it very often.

Both styles of parenting, I would propose, inform the child very quickly that it is not okay to simply be themselves. Coming back to this central tenant: when an individual begins to feel that it is unsafe to be themselves, they search for alternative ways to navigate the world that feel safe and manageable to them. This process of shapeshifting robs the individual of authenticity and empowerment.

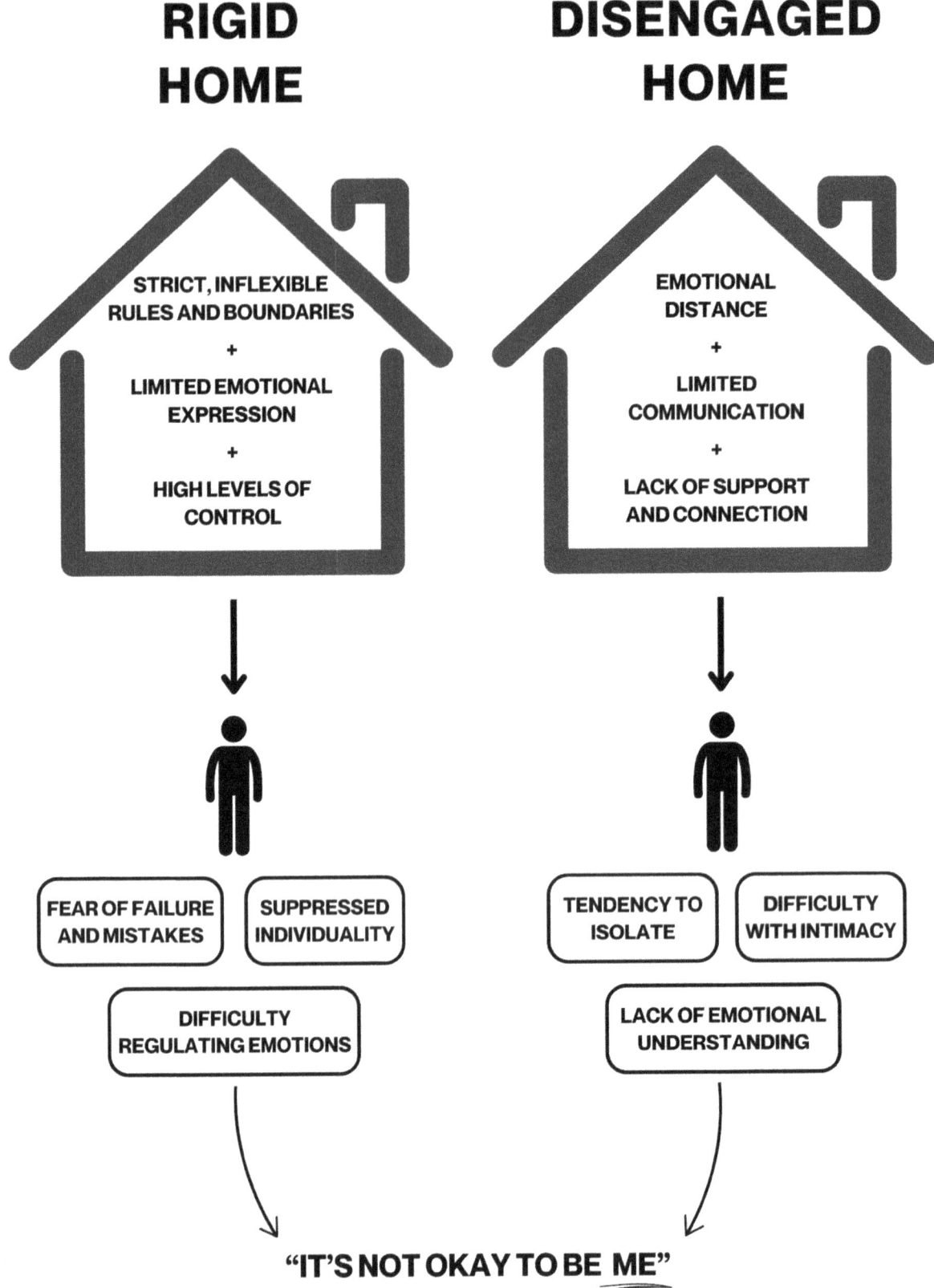

RELIGION

Religion can also play a significant part in problematic sexual behavior. While much of the research in the last decade has been rather mixed regarding problematic sexual behavior, it's clear that an individual's perception, when driven by religious dogma or ideology, has a positive correlation with damage to their present relationship, as those religious beliefs often drive disproportionate levels of shame and despair within the individual (Leonhardt et al., 2017).

Certainly, this is not meant to take a shot at religion. However, it is an attempt to highlight that one's perception/understanding, or rather, *lack* of understanding of their patterned behavior leads to a lack of agency and leaves them with internalization: placing blame on themselves for behaviors they do not understand.

Within this religious construct, one can maintain their faith or belief system so long as they can come to an understanding of their own destructive behavior patterns. There must be a comprehension of the underlying *need* in order to uncover new tools and insights for a healthy path forward. With this newfound awareness comes an ability to validate—not excuse—but validate *why* these destructive behaviors made sense at some time in one's life. This ability to understand historical patterns within oneself offers the opportunity to reverse engineer effective ways to meet the need.

Through this reverse engineering, one can understand historical "gaps" in terms of awareness and skills, using the knowledge of what *hasn't* worked to make healthier pathways for the future. Within this framework, it is certainly possible for faith and beliefs to exist and even play a significant role. Think of it like this: on top of understanding *why* I was engaging in historically destructive patterns, I can now validate myself simply by understanding why these patterns made sense—even if only on a chemical level. Then, one can layer their belief system on top of that, so as to help them garner even more strength, grace, and empowerment in moving forward.

Ultimately, the most important part is that the individual has now tossed aside internalization and shame, no longer solely blaming themselves for behavioral patterns that were previously not understood.

11

THE ROLE OF INTIMACY

As discussed in the previous chapter, this question around 'safety within the self' holds the very root of all intimacy dysfunction. I would propose that it is this *lack of safety (which includes truncated awareness)* that primarily drives dysfunctional sexual patterns. Simply put, I don't know myself, don't like myself, can't sit with myself, so I'm doing whatever is needed to get out form under this sensation/threat (which is myself).

> Typical addiction treatment then focuses solely on this behavior, however, the behavior was only a symptom from the person who's underlying driver was discomfort with the self. This goes light years beyond simply stating the pattern of behavior is a solution not a problem. Sure, it's a solution, but solution for what - escape from the self.

Intimacy, or human connection, is essential to our survival, and is one of the things that makes problematic sexual behavior so unique as an addictive pattern. If one's primary addiction is drinking alcohol, AA would famously tell them to "put a plug in the jug." Unfortunately, it's not quite that simple with intimacy. One cannot simply remove intimacy from their human experience, in the same way an individual battling an eating disorder cannot simply avoid food for the rest of their life.

The question and focus becomes, how does one get to a place where they feel safe being vulnerable? For many who navigate problematic sexual behavior, this dysfunctional behavior pattern originates at a time in their life when they did not feel safe to be themselves. Or, maybe more clearly, they feel that they constantly need to add or remove something from themselves to be accepted.

Most individuals who find themselves struggling with porn addiction, sex addiction, repeated infidelity, or other adjacent behavior patterns started out by seeking out safe, transactional, artificial intimacy. This **artificial intimacy** often mirrors the "real thing" and provides a veneer of safety, but prevents the individual from truly experiencing the connection, bonding, and security that comes with authentic intimacy and the "love drug," Oxytocin.

As I write this in 2025, we are now witnessing the rapid and exponential rise of artificial intelligence "companions," more commonly referred to as AI girlfriends/boyfriends. Since the Covid-19 pandemic, we've seen the "loneliness epidemic" emerge among younger generations. It's quite startling to see how these patterns are beginning to play out. From 2022 to 2024, the Google search term "AI girlfriend" increased by 2400%. The average user is a 27-year-old male, with 20% of men and 15% of women under the age of 28 having tested the waters of AI companionship.

I bring up AI companionship because it highlights the increasing drive to achieve transactional, safe intimacy with zero sense of risk for the individual *at that time*. However, of course, the greatest risk is to our multitude of muscles and synapses that allow our brains and bodies to navigate human interaction. Like any other muscle, they will eventually atrophy due to a lack of use. As we move increasingly toward a realm of transactional, artificial intimacy, we risk the loss of any and all connection, bonding, and safety that Oxytocin provides, effectively creating a new normal within our brains and bodies.

What previously felt slightly unsafe (a romantic interaction with the possibility of rejection) is now a sheer impossibility. The individual drives deeper into their safe, transactional cave, receiving constant and unending validation from their algorithm, which becomes more and more lifelike by the day.

Don't get me wrong: artificial intelligence is not to blame. Before artificial intelligence, transactional intimacy could still be achieved. Affairs, online chat rooms, cruising behaviors, adult movie theaters, one-night stands, strip clubs, escorts, porn binges—transactional and artificial intimacy is not a new concept. Artificial intelligence certainly threatens to take it to the next level, and has already begun to do so: 2024 saw $3.8 billion spent by American venture capital firms investing specifically in AI girlfriend company launches.

So while the players may be changing, the uniforms are still the same. The challenge for an individual who is trying to navigate these murky waters is ultimately to find a place where it is safe, OK, and dare I say, even beautiful to be themselves.

So, if the goal is to move in the direction of safe, vulnerable, relational intimacy, the following questions must be answered:

- What is my earliest memory of when it felt unsafe, or not OK, to simply be myself?

- When is the first time in my life that I can remember needing to escape, needing to get away?

- Why is vulnerability scary for me?

- When was I last able to be vulnerable with another person who I wouldn't want to reject me?

- Have my fears around being vulnerable ever come true?

- Which holds more weight for me: the fear of being rejected, or the excitement of being accepted?

- Have I ever found myself establishing transactional intimacy with my real-life romantic partners?

A great exercise here is **Core Beliefs**. One must understand their core beliefs, be able to track them, and then be able to challenge them with real-life, real-world data points to establish if one's core beliefs are true, or if they are simply trauma responses or fears that have never actually played out in one's life.

Core beliefs are a person's most central ideas about themselves, others, and the world. These beliefs act like a lens through which every situation and life experience is seen. Because of this, people with different core beliefs might be in the same situation but think, feel, and behave very differently. Even if a core belief is inaccurate, it still shapes how a person sees the world. Harmful core beliefs lead to negative thoughts, feelings, and behaviors, whereas rational core beliefs lead to balanced reactions.

Common Harmful Core Beliefs

I am unlovable
I am a loser
I am worthless
Nothing ever goes right for me

Consider how different core beliefs can affect one's interpretation of the same situation:

Situation: You meet someone new and think about asking them out for coffee.

I am not worthy → "Why would they ever go out with me?" → Does not ask the person out.

I am worthy → "We might have fun if we go out together." → Asks the person out to coffee.

As a person has new experiences, their core beliefs may gradually change. However, some experiences have a greater impact than others. Information that *supports* a core belief is easily integrated, making the belief stronger. Information that *does not* support a core belief tends to be ignored.

Here's an example of the exercise you'll be doing to examine and challenge your own core beliefs:

CORE BELIEFS EXERCISE

Core Belief: Nobody likes me.

Accepted
Information that supports my core belief.

- My friend didn't answer my phone call.

- The cashier at the grocery store was unfriendly.

- My boss gave me negative feedback at work.

Rejected
Information that does not support my core belief.

- I was invited to a coworker's birthday party.

- Customers at my job always seem happy to talk with me.

- My friend called to check in when I was sick.

Modified
Information I modified to support my core belief.

- I was asked out on a date… but it must have been out of pity.

- I'm close with my parents… but they're my parents, so they don't count.

- My friend gave me a birthday present… but only because I gave them one.

Coming to an understanding of your core beliefs and self-talk, and the rationality or irrationality of these beliefs, helps to understand the various cognitive distortions that can be at play and creating dysfunction. Now, complete the exercise using some of your core beliefs and examine the evidence collected.

CORE BELIEFS EXERCISE

Core Belief: _____

Accepted
Information that supports my core belief.

- _____

- _____

- _____

- _____

Rejected
Information that does not support my core belief.

- _____

- _____

- _____

- _____

Modified
Information modified to support my core belief.

- _____

- _____

- _____

- _____

CORE BELIEFS EXERCISE

Core Belief: _____

Accepted
Information that supports my core belief.

- _____

- _____

- _____

- _____

Rejected
Information that does not support my core belief.

- _____

- _____

- _____

- _____

Modified
Information modified to support my core belief.

- _____

- _____

- _____

- _____

CORE BELIEFS EXERCISE

Core Belief: _____

Accepted
Information that supports my core belief.

- _____

- _____

- _____

- _____

Rejected
Information that does not support my core belief.

- _____

- _____

- _____

- _____

Modified
Information modified to support my core belief.

- _____

- _____

- _____

- _____

12

BEWARE RECOVERY FATIGUE
THE LAW OF DIMINISHING RETURNS

Just as with all good things, eventually there will be an inevitable tipping point where rest, or acclimatization is necessary. One cannot run at top speed indefinitely. The same is true for achieving sustainable sexual integrity.

This chapter is simply to help you become aware - or if you've already experienced recovery fatigue to validate you - recovery fatigue will arrive along your journey at some point or another. This is nothing to fret over or worry about, it is simply a part of the process.

The more important question, then, is what would recovery fatigue look like for you?

I would propose that recovery fatigue is outwardly noticeable when you stop engaging in parts of your 'process' that before you found truly helpful. The VALUE in the activity has diminished to a place where it is no longer worth the time, effort or energy to engage with it.

Understanding that this will happen, gird your loins - to borrow a phrase - and be prepared to experience this recovery fatigue phenomenon as well as being prepared to respond. What will you do? There is no right answer, simply increasing awareness will prove incredibly helpful at this stage.

FINAL THOUGHTS

∼

I want to commend you on making it to the end of this workbook. Clearly, you've shown an incredible level of engagement and intentionality - authenticity is clearer, bringing empowerment not imprisonment.

As you move forward, remember your past patterns were not a problem, but a solution to an unmet need. Moving ahead and beyond this workbook, you will continue to find new ways to meet your own ever-changing needs, ways to feel safe within yourself, and continually grow in your own understanding of those needs that arise within. This is a lifelong process.

A couple key points worth taking away with you...
- It's safe to be you
- Healthy drives sober, not the other way around
- You live a life of presence, not absence
- You are able to operate & communicate from a space of vulnerability
- You have a clearly defined & documented process; preventative and acute
- You love your younger self - there is no self-hatred
- You know your 'why'
- You know your 'how'
- You are empowered, not fearful or hopeful, in your sexual integrity
- Your identity, value & worth are not tied into your 'streak'

I would propose that the most important part of a sustainable, sexual integrity pathway is one of self-awareness, self-efficacy, and one that commonly breaks isolation. I don't know if you, or anyone, will ever fully and completely "figure this out." Your understanding, your skills, your responsiveness to yourself and others, and your ability to bounce back — all of these things will grow and develop, maturing over time, continually evolving you into healthier and healthier positions, in both process and outcome. However, I would warn you, that the day you believe you have "figured it out" may be the day that you stop considering new, improved, deeper ideas.

And now we celebrate. We celebrate your beginnings, we celebrate the present (the only place we truly have power), and we celebrate the unknown future and all that it will bring - both roses and thorns.

    Continue celebrating.
    Strong work.

YOUR NOTES
FEEL FREE TO TAKE AS MANY NOTES AS YOU'D LIKE IN THIS SECTION

YOUR TOP 3 TAKEAWAYS FROM THE WORKBOOK:

1. ...
2. ...
3. ...

∼

All notes...

DATE:

DATE:

DATE:

DATE:

DATE:

DATE:

DATE:

YOUR NOTES

DATE:

DATE:

DATE:

DAILY CHECK-IN TEMPLATE

TODAY'S DATE:

    1-10 Scale _____ **Transparent %** _____ **Fantasy %** _____

What is my intention? _____
How will I break isolation? _____
How will I practice presence? _____

Gratitude List

1. _____

2. _____

3. _____

4. _____

5. _____

Affirmations

1. _____

2. _____

3. _____

Process Tweak?

_____

_____

_____

_____

ABOUT THE AUTHOR

Blair is husband and father first and foremost. He was born in Thomasville, GA but grew up just outside of Boston, MA which is where he also currently resides.

Blair has enjoyed working as a 'helper', having started out as a Certified Nurse Assistant working the bedside for many years, with his first Mental Health Counseling role at the Arbour Hospital in Jamaica Plain, Massachusetts in 2001. Since then Blair has worked on both the clinical, administrative, research, academic and start-up side of healthcare in both non-profit and for-profit environments, but his true passion has always been one-on-one individual work with clients navigating addiction.

Blair has worked as an addiction counselor on locked inpatient detox units, step-down detox units, Partial Hospitalization Programs, Intensive Outpatient Programs, Methadone Clinics, night shift at a Level 1 Trauma Center Emergency Department as well as in private practice. Blair continues to work as an adjunct faculty at two universities in Boston, Suffolk University and Massachusetts College of Pharmacy & Health Sciences. He serves as an advisory board member at Suffolk University's Healthcare Administration Department and former advisory board member at Harvard Medical School (Center for Primary Care). Blair also worked on the team to launch Amazon Care, was Chief Operating Officer at Sturdy Health and ran the Division of General Medicine at one of the largest Harvard teaching hospitals in Boston, Beth Israel Deaconess Medical Center downtown where he was responsible for 60,000 patients in primary care, palliative care and research.

Blair has spoken nationally on such topics as "Artificial Intimacy & AI Companionship" at Nashville, Tennessee's Compulsive Sexual Behavior Conference and "Hitting the Triple Aim: Healthier Patients, Happier Patients at a Lower Cost of Care" at Austin, Texas' Medical Group Manager's Association Annual Conference.

Blair is a board-certified National Certified Counselor® (NCC) having successfully completed the National Clinical Mental Health Counselor exam (NCMHCE) awarded by the National Board for Certified Counselors and maintains a concentration in Sustainable Sexual Integrity working with those meeting criteria for Compulsive Sexual Behavior Disorder, he's a Certified Sexual Addiction Therapist candidate with the International Institute for Trauma &

Addiction Professionals, he holds two Masters degrees (in Clinical Mental Health Counseling and Health Administration), is a member of both the American Counseling Association and International Institute for Trauma & Addiction Professionals.

instagram.com/bpbcounseling
linkedin.com/in/blairbisher
youtube.com/@bpbcounseling

REFERENCES

- Raihan, N., & Cogburn, M. (2023). *Stages of change theory*. PubMed; StatPearls Publishing. https://www.ncbi.nlm.nih.gov/books/NBK556005/
- Volkow, N. D., Michaelides, M., & Baler, R. (2019). The neuroscience of drug reward and addiction. *Physiological Reviews*, 99(4), 2115–2140. https://doi.org/10.1152/physrev.00014.2018
- Larimer, M. E., Palmer, R. S., & Marlatt, G. A. (1999). Relapse prevention. An overview of Marlatt's cognitive-behavioral model. *Alcohol research & health : the journal of the National Institute on Alcohol Abuse and Alcoholism*, 23(2), 151–160
- Bőthe, B., Tóth-Király, I., Zsila, Á., Griffiths, M. D., Demetrovics, Z., & Orosz, G. (2018). The Development of the Problematic Pornography Consumption Scale (PPCS). *Journal of sex research*, 55(3), 395–406. https://doi.org/10.1080/00224499.2017.1291798
- Grant, J. E., Potenza, M. N., Weinstein, A., & Gorelick, D. A. (2010). Introduction to behavioral addictions. *The American Journal of Drug and Alcohol Abuse*, 36(5), 233–241. https://doi.org/10.3109/00952990.2010.491884
- Grubbs, J. B., Kraus, S. W., & Perry, S. L. (2019). Self-reported addiction to pornography in a nationally representative sample: The roles of use habits, religiousness, and moral incongruence. *Journal of Behavioral Addictions*, 8(1), 88–93. https://doi.org/10.1556/2006.7.2018.134
- Beáta Bőthe, István Tóth-Király, Zsolt Demetrovics, & Orosz, G. (2021). Problematic Pornography Consumption Scale--Short Version. *PsycTESTS Dataset*. https://doi.org/10.1037/t79815-000

- Mirjam A Tuk, Sonja Prokopec, Bram Van den Bergh, Do versus Don't: The Impact of Framing on Goal-Level Setting, *Journal of Consumer Research*, Volume 47, Issue 6, April 2021, Pages 1003–1024, https://doi.org/10.1093/jcr/ucaa050
- Šoková, B., Greškovičová, K., Halamová, J., & Baránková, M. (2025). Breaking the vicious cycles of self-criticism: a qualitative study on the best practices of overcoming one's inner critic. *BMC psychology*, 13(1), 266. https://doi.org/10.1186/s40359-024-02250-2

www.ingramcontent.com/pod-product-compliance
Lightning Source LLC
Chambersburg PA
CBHW080550030426
42337CB00024B/4820